Ritchie Valens
THE FIRST LATINO ROCKER

Bilingual Press/Editorial Bilingüe

General Editor
Gary D. Keller

Managing Editor
Karen S. Van Hooft

Senior Editor
Mary M. Keller

Assistant Editor
Linda Thurston

Address
Bilingual Review/Press
Hispanic Research Center
Arizona State University
Tempe, Arizona 85287
(602) 965-3867

Ritchie Valens

THE FIRST LATINO ROCKER

BEVERLY MENDHEIM

c. 1

Bilingual Press/Editorial Bilingüe
TEMPE, ARIZONA

B
VALENS, R

ISBN: 0-916950-79-4

Library of Congress Catalog Card Number: 87-71700

PRINTED IN THE UNITED STATES OF AMERICA

Cover illustration by Bill Fergusson

Cover design by Christopher J. Bidlack

Back cover photo by Boldman Studios, Seattle

TABLE OF CONTENTS

vălens -entis (partic. from vălĕo, *to be strong*), adj. *strong, powerful*
 —From *Cassell's New Latin Dictionary*. New York: Funk & Wagnalls, 1960.

1

INTRODUCTION

The year 1958 was musically exciting for me. After a two to three-year hiatus, I "came back" to rock and roll, not knowing at the time why. Looking back, I can now see that Black rhythm and blues, renamed "rock and roll" by Alan Freed, a Cleveland disc jockey transplanted to New York, became "whitewashed" regardless of whether it was sung by Elvis Presley or Pat Boone. By 1958, it seemed to me that rock and roll was equally balanced with Black as well as white talent. I became a fervent viewer of Dick Clark's "American Bandstand" and Alan Freed's TV show. It was as much a part of me as going to Mass on Sundays and occasional weekdays. Although my eleven-year-old tastes still adhered to novelties such as "The Witch Doctor," "The Purple People Eater" and even the "Chipmunk Song," the air waves were fortunately rich with teen idols who performed *real* rock and roll, rockers like Bobby Darin, Jackie Wilson, the Everly Brothers, Duane Eddy and Bobby Freeman, to name a few. And there was plenty of variety: teen ballads, chalypso, doo-wop, girl/boy duos, rockabilly, novelty, and, for lack of a better term, just plain ol' rock 'n' roll!

One evening early in September, 1958, when I tuned into the Alan Freed radio show on WINS from my tenement apartment in the central Bronx, a song came on that was to change my life in a very special way. It was customary among my schoolmates at the fairly integrated Catholic school I attended to play a guessing game about whether a new song that came out by a singer or group was sung by Blacks or whites. We were seventh and eighth graders and the majority of us who were Black or Puerto Rican were hardly fooled by an increasing effort on the part of white performers to sound as "colored" as possible. In the beginning, Bobby Darin had many of us guessing! Indeed, that memorable night when I first heard the song "Come On, Let's Go" by Ritchie

Valens, I was deeply puzzled. He sounded neither Black nor white. Since I had been exposed extensively to Latin music, I could detect a certain Latin quality in his singing and I suspected that he just might be "Spanish." My puzzlement was not resolved when I saw him perform on "American Bandstand," for what I saw was an obviously heavy-set "white" boy with few of what I then considered to be Hispanic features, although a later picture in a fan magazine once again aroused my suspicion, not to mention Ritchie's second release, an obviously Latin song, "La Bamba." Nobody was saying a word and unless one was from the southern California area, no one *knew* that Ritchie Valens was of Mexican-American heritage—not until after his death. I remember two Hispanic schoolmates arguing in the schoolyard about whether Ritchie was Spanish, meaning that his family was originally from Spain, or Mexican, meaning originally from Mexico. This clandestine attitude of the 50's gave way to later writings that Valens was of "Mexican-Indian" heritage which is not altogether correct. To say that the fair-complexioned, hazel-eyed boy who often wore his dark hair in a perfect 50's "waterfall" was *mestizo*, as is true of most people of Mexican heritage, would have been more correct.

Furthermore, as far as I can remember, Ritchie never sang "La Bamba" on "American Bandstand," nor "The Dick Clark Saturday Show," nor even the more "liberal" Alan Freed weekly TV show, even though "La Bamba" reached No. 22 on the *Billboard* charts, while its flip side, "Donna," went all the way to No. 2. (The two-sided release was considered a double-sided hit, a rare occurrence in rock music even to this day.) "La Bamba" was also not performed at the Christmas show of 1958, held at Loew's State Theater in New York, where by chance I had the opportunity to see Valens in person. I remember being truly amazed at the beauty of his voice when he sang the simple teen ballad "Donna" which he had composed. Unlike many of my contemporaries, I never fell head over heels for a teen idol—that is, not until I saw Ritchie Valens. It was during "The Music Shop," a Sunday variety TV show hosted by Buddy Bregman, January 17, 1959, that I became infatuated with Valens and saw that he was much too talented to go unrecognized. It was then that I decided to buy his records, join his fan club and see him again when he came to town. Ritchie Valens had joined the ranks as a teen idol, at least for me.

*   *   *

I remember February 3, 1958, as a cold, miserable Tuesday in New York. I wore an emerald green skirt with a kick pleat, a short-sleeved blue pullover with black and white stripes and warm black tights, instead of my drab school uniform—a navy blue skirt and long-sleeved white blouse. The boiler had broken that day so there was no school. I was doing my math homework when news of a plane crash in which Ritchie Valens had been killed came over WINS radio. I kept the radio and TV news on for the rest of the day, hoping against hope that the reports were wrong. After watching "American Bandstand" and later listening to the Alan Freed radio show, on which Alan played Roy Hamilton's "You'll Never Walk Alone" as a tribute to the three stars, I was finally convinced that I had lost the one and only teen idol I ever had.

*   *   *

At the time of Ritchie Valens' death, UPI listed him first, "the seventeen-year-old recording sensation," before Buddy Holly or J.P. Richardson, the "Big Bopper." Valens was hailed as "the next Presley" and, shortly thereafter, there came a surge of movie and teen-magazine stories on his life. Memorial fan clubs were started for Ritchie in both the U.S. and Europe. Tribute shows around the southern California area were given, culminating in an eventful Ritchie Valens Memorial Concert, held New Year's Eve, 1961, at the Long Beach Civic Auditorium, at which the Beach Boys made their debut. Yet, despite it all, most literature on the history of rock and roll either ignores Ritchie Valens or treats him as a footnote—"the singer who died with Buddy Holly." A few rock historians, such as Griel Marcus, Charlie Gillett and the late Lester Bangs, have recognized the importance of Valens' music and his contributions to the world of rock. Within the last five years, there has been a renewed effort on the part of various writers, mostly within California circles, to rediscover him.

Why is Ritchie Valens important? In addition to the fact that he was actually the first successful Chicano rock and roller, the music he produced made him the "father" of Latin/Chicano rock. Indeed, some of his contributions which until now have remained fairly unknown extend beyond his being the "father" of a music. His music was one of the first to combine elements of rock and jazz; Ritchie was, along with Duane Eddy and Eddie Cochran, a developer of the "garage band" sound (actually originating with Bo Diddley), which contributed to what later became known as "surf music." He was one of the first rockers to use the idea of a medley of melodies within a song (often called "through-composed" in traditional music circles), and he was one of the first to use assymetrical rhythms and pentatonic (five-tone) melodies, previously confined to Black urban blues. Amazingly, all of this making of musical history was accomplished through a few songs and song fragments that barely filled three albums, in a period of less than eight months, by a seventeen-year-old boy!

Back in 1969 in a *Rolling Stone* article, Griel Marcus said, "Valens sang fragile melodies with the enthusiasm and commitment of Little Richard, and the tension that resulted from the fusion of these two elements in a single song captivated his audience and made him a star." Rock historian Charlie Gillett also recognized Valens' importance in his 1970 book, *The Sound of the City: The Rise of Rock and Roll*, and said, "Although no distinctive 'West Coast' style of rock had developed with any of the four important former rhythm 'n' blues [recording] companies [Alladin, Modern, Specialty and Imperial], a style that was identified particularly with California did develop, showing the strong influence of Mexican rhythms. The most successful singer of this style was Ritchie Valens." That same year Lester Bangs wrote in *Rolling Stone* about the Pacoima Junior High School album: "Valens sang with an unassuming sincerity that made him more truly touching than any other artist . . . from his era." Later, in the 1981 revision of *The Rolling Stone Illustrated History of Rock 'n' Roll*, Bangs added that Valens' "La Bamba" was one of the first examples of punk rock. In his chapter "Protopunk: The Garage Bands," Bangs said, "Just consider Valens' three-chord mariachi square-up [on "La Bamba"] in the light of 'Louie, Louie' by the Kingsmen, then 'You Really Got Me' by the Kinks, and then 'No Fun' by the Stooges, then 'Blitzkrieg Bop' by the Ramones, and finally note that 'Blitzkrieg Bop' by the Ramones sounds a lot like 'La Bamba.' There: Twenty years of rock and roll history in three chords played more primitively each time they are recycled."

"La Bamba" and other songs initially recorded by Ritchie Valens have been revised over the years by numerous rock, folk and country artists, notables such as Led Zeppelin, Freddy Fender, Donny Osmond, Ronnie Hawkins, the post-Holly Crickets, and the Ramones, to name a few. Yet Valens' recordings remained inaccessible especially in the U.S. where the last American release was an MGM "greatest hits" package back in 1969. It was only in 1981 that Rhino re-issued Valens' music, thanks to the efforts of a local Los Angeles writer Jim Dawson. In the meantime, Valens' music was available in European circles, and albums of various quality could be found in England, Germany, Holland and France. For almost twelve years the musical memory of Ritchie Valens had been forgotten in rock and roll America.

I began my research into the making of this book back in 1970. It was a year in which rock and roll began to look at its roots. Upon refreshing my memory with Valens' recordings, I was determined to at least try to restore the history of his music. But personal obligations and other interests made it impossible for me to continue the project. I resumed the project in 1978 and have done the bulk of the research since then. I used as resources Ritchie's family, relatives and friends, including the members of the Silhouettes, a group Ritchie joined before coming to the attention of manager Bob Keane (formerly, Keene); Bob Keane and sessions musicians from Del-Fi; other musicians that either played or associated with Valens, as well as performers contemporary with Ritchie; teachers at Pacoima Junior High School; local Los Angeles disc jockeys; and others in the Valens story. Memories from twenty-five years ago or earlier were relayed to me to the extent that they could be recalled. There may be points in this book at which the reader will wonder about the availability of additional or conclusive information on nonmusical as well as musical aspects of Ritchie's life. In these instances information was no doubt either lost or scanty in people's memories or it was conflicting. When I found disagreement, I tried to present all sides and offer resolutions if possible.

The purpose of this book is to tell the story of a very unique individual, who rose from the poverty of a Los Angeles barrio to become a musical phenomenon. I have devoted most of the text to the musical experiences of Ritchie Valens and to the factors that shaped those experiences. Therefore, this book is primarily a documentation of the *musical* rather than the *social* history of Ritchie Valens and is not intended to be an official biography, but rather a permanent memorial to one who died so young yet so talented.

I am especially grateful to those who have given their time and assistance in relating their accounts of Ritchie Valens, primarily Ernestine and Eliodoro Reyes (Ritchie's aunt and uncle). I am also thankful to Gilbert Rocha for contacting many of Valens' acquaintances, as well as for relating his own personal experiences. I am equally grateful to all of the following people who have offered their memories of Ritchie Valens and of their associations with him: Concepción Valenzuela (Ritchie's mother), Robert Morales (Ritchie's older brother), Richard Cota (deceased), John Rico, David Chaubet, Lillian Rocha-Beckett and Donna Ludwig Fox; members of the Silhouettes, Bill and Conrad Jones, Walter Takaki, Frankie Gallardo, Armando Ortiz, Walter Préndez (deceased) and Freddie Aguilera; Ritchie's teachers at Pacoima Junior High, John Whitaker, Paul Omatsu and Ernie Brandt, and former principal David Schwartz; manager Bob Keane; orchestrator Rene Hall; sessions musicians and other musical associates, Earl Palmer, Red Collender, Carol Kaye, Ernie Freeman (deceased), Stan Ross, Ted Quillin, Bill Angel, Elliot Field, Stan Beverly (a.k.a. Rayce Gentry), Carter Saxon, Chuck Blore, Sharon Sheeley, Bo Diddley, Jimmy Clanton, Dick Dale, Ian Whitcomb and Freddy Fender, and members of Los Lobos, César Rosas, David Hidalgo, Conrad Lozano, Luis Pérez and Steve Berlin; school friends, Chuck Armendáriz, Gail González-Smith, Judy Hoyt, John Alcaraz, Manny Sandoval, Doug Macchia, Louis Raring, Jerry Faulkner and Joseph Tovar.

Those whose assistance should also be acknowledged are: Bill Griggs, Jim Dawson, Tom Powell, John Goldrosen, Derek Glenister, Deter Boek, Gerd Muesfeldt, Ragnar Ebsen, Gary King, Barry Pollack, Kathy Turner, Steve Propes, Robert Sterelcyzk, Larry Matti, Don Larson, Bill Fergusson, Barbara Rau, and Dr. Lawrence Estrada.

Perhaps the person to whom I owe my deepest gratitude is Salvador Gutiérrez. Without his untiring assistance in collecting many of the interviews and other research materials, this book would have been incomplete in many respects. It is to Salvador, to Ritchie's family and to my family that I dedicate this book.

2

"The Boy from Pacoima . . .
and San Fernando"

Which community could claim Ritchie Valens as its own: Los Angeles, San Fernando, Pacoima? The truth is Ritchie's short life focused on all of them—he was born in Los Angeles, raised and attended school in both San Fernando and Pacoima—and performed in virtually every major area of the Los Angeles and surrounding southern California counties.

The county of Los Angeles consists of the city of Los Angeles and several unincorporated small communities. Each of these communities has a history and a way of life of its own with a distinct ethnic makeup and a separate industrial and commercial base. The same is true of the San Fernando and neighboring Pacoima, both located about twenty-one miles northwest of downtown Los Angeles at the edge of the San Fernando Valley.

Of the two, San Fernando is more renowned because of its nickname, "The Mission City." It was independently established as a city in 1874, one and one-half miles east of the Mission San Fernando del Rey España, founded almost a century earlier by a successor of Junípero Serra, the original Catholic missionary father to the California missions. While under the Mexican flag, a community of Indians, Spaniards and Mexicans prospered in and around the Valley which took its namesake from the Mission. Around 1842, gold was discovered just north of the Valley and U.S. citizens began to pour into the area. After the Mexican War of 1846–7, California was annexed to the United States.

The Mission community had created a highly developed irrigation system and, as a result, San Fernando's industry remained basically agricultural: Citrus fruits, especially oranges, became and remained the town's main crop. The introduction of the Southern Pacific Railway in the 1880's was an asset in connecting the town with the rest of the Valley, as well as with Los Angeles and southern California in general. Small businesses began to develop and the population continued to grow. San Fernando High School was established in 1896, being the first high school in the Valley and the second in the Los Angeles vicinity. A series of droughts at the turn of the century may have been a major reason why San Fernando, along with other towns in the Valley, voted jointly to annex to the City of Los Angeles in 1915 for the purpose of receiving additional water supplies. San Fernando's Hispanic community, influential from the start, increased considerably by way of migrations of Mexican-Americans into the southern California area as a whole. By 1950, the "Mission City's" population was mostly of Mexican heritage. Today San Fernando contains a population of about 18,000 and incorporates about two and one-half square miles. The City as it presently exists is totally renewed, with many of its "downtown" buildings reflecting its Hispanic heritage. This renewal occurred in the wake of an earthquake which struck the Los Angeles area in February, 1971. Sylmar, a community near San Fernando, was the epicenter of this quake which destroyed a considerable part of the business district of the "Mission City."

Lying immediately east of San Fernando is Pacoima, a semi-rural community which has evolved into a suburb within the last thirty to forty years. Pacoima takes its name from the Gabrielino Indian language meaning "rushing waters" referring to the periodic floods to the north in Pacoima Canyon. The Toneva or Tujunga Indians would avoid the floods by settling in the area below the Canyon where present-day Pacoima is located. Though sixteen square miles larger, Pacoima in many ways shared the history of the Mission San Fernando and its later town. Activities and social life in Pacoima have centered around San Fernando even to the present day. When Pacoima residents talk of "going into town," they mean the "Mission City," not Los Angeles. Pacoima developed a small agricultural industry, mostly olives, and has boasted a small lumber industry since 1921. A 1923 song "I Love You Pacoima" by G. Allison Phelps reflected its then still rural and idyllic setting, which attracted western stars during the 40's and 50's, although this environment was rapidly fading by the time Ritchie was born.

San Fernando and Pacoima both share a strong Latino heritage and both in Ritchie's time were virtually the only areas in the

Valley that had integrated populations of Hispanics (mostly of Mexican heritage), Blacks, Asians and whites. Judging by attendance at Pacoima Junior High and San Fernando High, there were considerably more whites residing in the two towns during Ritchie's time than today when the ethnic population of both Pacoima and San Fernando is predominantly Chicano.

As previously mentioned, Americans of Mexican descent have long been established in California. Over the years, migrations from other southwestern states and Mexico have doubled if not tripled the Hispanic population of Los Angeles County. Ritchie's father, Joseph Steve Valenzuela, was a native of California; his mother, Concepción Reyes, was born in Arizona and came to California with her family to settle with relations already established in the San Fernando/Pacoima area.

Joseph Steve (called Steve by his acquaintances) was by profession a tree surgeon, but also worked at a variety of jobs, including mining and training horses. In 1941, both Steve and his wife Concepción (called Connie by her acquaintances), who was expecting, were working at a munitions factory in Saugus, just north of San Fernando. Connie already had another son, then four years old, named Robert Morales, from a previous marriage. On May 12, 1941, around late afternoon, Steve rushed his wife to Los Angeles County Osteopathic Hospital located on north Mission Road in Los Angeles, where she delivered a son at 12:56 A.M., May 13th. The couple named their child Richard Steve.

At the time of Ritchie's birth, the Valenzuelas were living in San Fernando, at 1337 Coronel Street, not far from the Southern Pacific Railroad. Like the surrounding families, they had only the bare essentials. Sometime before he was three, Ritchie's parents separated, and Ritchie spent most of his time with his father, who bought some property on Fillmore Street in Pacoima. But the separation was hardly complete for the couple would continue to see each other on occasion.

David Chaubet, who lived next door to Ritchie as a child and was one of Ritchie's first playmates, remembered much about Ritchie's father: "Steve was kind of a hard-boiled person. He had an accident—a mining explosion—a natural gas leak which blew up on him. He got pretty well torn up . . . my dad and [Ritchie's] dad didn't get along, my dad was a mechanic and he never fixed Steve's car right and they used to fight over it. So what Ritchie and I used to do was dig tunnels in the backyard [to play with each other] and then cover them up. Steve was this type of guy: He used to sit at the house and call me, 'You starving Okie! Come over here and sit down to eat!' and I'd say, 'I don't wanna eat, Steve,' and he'd say, 'I don't wanna eat alone!' He would even come out, get ahold of me, put me down at the table and say, 'Now, you're gonna eat when you're with me!'"

Chaubet recalled another side of Steve—that of a strict yet caring father who always provided for his son, often spoiling him. Steve had intense feelings about Ritchie's musical talents. He wanted Ritchie to make something of himself and encouraged him to learn how to play a musical instrument, particularly the guitar, but also the trumpet, as well as to keep up his singing. Ritchie never learned how to play the guitar very well until he entered junior high school. Said Chaubet, "Ritchie sang since he was a child. As he got older, his voice got better. He used to sing a lot of country-western. He was a natural, born with a talent. I have seen guys study [music] for years and if they ain't got it, they ain't got it! Richard did have it.

"Steve used to throw some good-sized parties and a lot of times Ritchie would be embarrassed [to sing] and didn't want to do it. Then his dad would take out his goddamn belt and say, 'You better do it or I'll see that you gonna get it!' Then [Ritchie] would do it."

As a child, Ritchie had western heroes, singing cowboys such as Roy Rogers and Gene Autry. Whether or not he actually saw them appear in person is not known. However, alongside his desire to be a "singing cowboy," Ritchie also had a love for horses. Occasionally, Steve would work at a ranch in Piru Valley, a few miles north of Pacoima in Ventura County, and would take Ritchie along. As a small child, Ritchie liked to ride on a sheep and pretend it was a horse, but as he got older, he rode horses, not only in Piru Valley but also around the Pacoima/San Fernando area. A neighbor and close friend of Ritchie's, Lillian Rocha-Beckett, recalled, "He [Ritchie] used to tell me that someday he was going to have enough money to buy a ranch and have a lot of horses."

Several sources have stated that Joseph Steve died of diabetes in 1951, when Ritchie was ten years old. He may have died of this, although Chaubet believed he died of a stroke—from a ruptured sac under the heart. He said, "Steve was pretty sick there in the last few years."

What happened to Ritchie after Steve died is somewhat confusing. Connie moved into Steve's house, located at 13058 Fillmore St. in Pacoima, with her older son, Robert, and two very young daughters, Connie (junior) and Irma. Yet Robert (Bob) Morales recalled that Ritchie did not come back to live with them until age eleven. Sometime before entering Pacoima Junior High, Ritchie did stay with an uncle in Norwalk, California, and another uncle, Henry Felix, in Santa Monica. Some unreliable sources from fan magazines stated that his residence in Santa Monica with that uncle was because of his "running wild" shortly after his father died. Although Pacoima at the time was beginning to gain a reputation for being a tough neighborhood, hardly anyone could ever recall Ritchie being a wild kid. One former schoolmate at Pacoima Elementary remembered him as a kid who was not loud or noticeable. Like many families of Hispanic heritage, the Valenzuelas and the Reyes (Ritchie's mother's side) were extended families and living indefinitely with uncles, aunts, grandparents or cousins was not uncommon. Ritchie's maternal grandmother, Refugia Reyes, stayed with his mother after his grandfather, Frank, died in 1957. In some respects Ritchie was more of a "Reyes" than a "Valenzuela" in that he associated more with his mother's relatives even when his father was alive.

Several of these relatives were responsible for Ritchie's early exposure to music. One relative supposedly helped him make a toy guitar from a cigar box when he was five years old (His mother even remembered his attempting to make one from a can and rubber bands at the age of three!). His cousin Richard "Dickie" Cota also played the guitar, being Ritchie's main exposure to Latin songs, and may have been the originator of the beginning guitar riff Ritchie used on "La Bamba." His uncle John Lozano taught Ritchie some of the chords of the guitar. The same unreliable sources from fan magazines mentioned earlier stated that Ritchie's father was a "Latin guitarist" and that Steve gave his son a guitar at the age of nine. Steve may have given Ritchie a guitar then, but had Steve been a guitarist himself he certainly would have taught Ritchie some chords. Steve may have played the guitar when he was young but may have forgotten. There also may have been relations on Ritchie's father's side who played the guitar, but assuredly Ritchie received lessons by the time he was eleven or twelve from Lozano.

Once Ritchie got into the guitar, he would find a quiet room in the house and practice for hours without going out, but while in elementary school, Ritchie did not take his guitar with him to school as he did later in junior high.

Besides Pacoima Elementary, Ritchie attended Haddon Elementary also in Pacoima, Carmelita School while in Norwalk and an elementary school in Santa Monica. Although his parents were Catholic, Ritchie did not attend Catholic school because even at that time the schools may have been overcrowded or the tuition too expensive for his family to afford. Ritchie lived in several places which accounts for his attending different schools. A former Pacoima Elementary schoolmate, a Chicana who wished not to be identified, recalled Ritchie as a "pudgy, light-complexioned kid who was never an 'A' or 'B' pupil, just passing grade." She had a particular story she remembered of Ritchie: "When we were in grammar school, Ritchie happened to like me but I didn't care for him because he was poor. I had a birthday party and we lived behind this dump. It was the kind of dump you could walk around and find things that were broken and pick up . . . [Ritchie] went to the dump [and] brought me a bracelet. I gave it back to him. Later, my mother was so mad at me and I felt so bad afterwards. I had really hurt him. After that, he was sort of distant. When we met again in high school, he remembered but he never took it out on me, nothing like that."

Pacoima Junior High School

Pacoima Junior High School opened its doors for the first time on September 19, 1954. Ritchie entered the school in the seventh grade at the age of thirteen. The plant of the school was not yet completed so classes were held temporarily on the campus of San Fernando Junior High in San Fernando. Around January 5, 1955, Pacoima Junior High moved permanently to Laurel Canyon Boulevard in Pacoima.

Ernie Brandt, one of the veteran teachers of Pacoima Junior High, recounted his first meeting with Ritchie:

"I remember him coming into the room with a big cut across either his left or right arm. He looked like a knife fighter or something and I thought, 'Oh, boy! That's probably a rough kid!'

But he was quiet and orderly. He seemed to do his work well and later on I discovered he had a beautiful sense of humor . . . Ritchie had a few difficulties here and there. I thought he was an average student, if I remember correctly. He tried pretty hard and I don't think he ever skipped class when I had him . . . he was, in my opinion, a fine person all around, a good example to set. He brightened up our days here."

Brandt clearly remembered Ritchie carrying a guitar and playing it during school breaks and at lunchtime, as well as at school functions, sometimes solo, other times with two or three boys. "Everybody listened to him," said Brandt. "They'd enjoy his jokes or he would take a song and paraphrase it. There was one song, 'Davy Crockett,' which he would change to a very humorous song. Later on, at a program, Ritchie and three other boys got together to sing a trio of it."

John Whitaker, the industrial arts teacher, indicated that his woodshop class was probably Ritchie's favorite class. He recalled, "Ritchie had several older guitars that he wanted to refinish which he did in class. It took an abnormally long time because he really treated them like they were his babies." Whitaker's class was also another opportunity to play the guitar, for acoustic purposes, if not merely for enjoyment. Said Whitaker, "When I said, 'Ritchie, there's a time and place for everything. This is not the time to play the guitar. Let's get busy,' he would put it away. But you know, he would wait and play it until I got to that point."

In those days, there were bleachers in the back of the school and Ritchie used to sit at the top of them with a group of other students, always singing and playing his guitar. "As teachers," said Whitaker, "we would always look out for little knots of kids, thinking, 'Oh! Oh! Another fight!' But when Ritchie was involved, it was always a group of kids listening to him and the teachers allowed it because he was so good at it." Former principal David Schwartz recalled some of the teachers asking him whether such gatherings centered around Ritchie were permissible, fearing such a crowd could get out of hand. "I talked with Ritchie about it," said Schwartz. "We had an understanding that as long as everything was okay and there were no problems, he could continue to do that."

Former schoolmate Joseph Tovar was in the same grade as Ritchie and remembered him as an average student who did better in English than most of his peers. "We would get together and study," said Tovar. "In math, [Ritchie] had his low point; he would ask other peers who had the ability, but in crafts, he was an artist. He was able to do things with his hands, to form plastic into beautiful figurines." (It is possible that these crafts no longer survive because of a fire in 1961 which destroyed Ritchie's family's house.) "We also used to play baseball after school together," added Tovar.

The student body of Pacoima Junior High reflected its surrounding neighborhood: mostly white with a mixture of Blacks, Chicanos, and a few Asians, mostly of Japanese descent. Tolerance was the general norm of things, although veteran teachers at Pacoima remembered the white youths being more unruly and prone to violence than any other ethnic group. Racial confrontation existed but probably not as often as in other neighborhoods. When it happened, it was usually outside the campus, or between specific members of a white or Chicano gang. Groups tended to associate with each other based on what neighborhood they came from, rather than what color skin they had. Students generally minded their own business and avoided troublemakers; in this respect, Ritchie was no different.

Local Chicano kids at Pacoima Junior High during the 50's did not speak Spanish among themselves as often as in later times, to the extent that there was a concern for bilingualism in the schools. When Spanish was used, it was usually local Spanish colloquialisms or slang mixed with English spoken among peers or Spanish spoken with family members. Although Ritchie spoke little Spanish (his brother Robert recalled he did not speak Spanish at all until after he came to live with his mother), he was obliged to do so with his grandparents and especially his grandmother who spoke no English at all.

A description of Ritchie at Pacoima Junior High would have been of a slightly heavy-set boy, with a fair complexion and hazel-green eyes, who wore old levis or "peggers" with a "Sir Guy" shirt and would occasionally wear his coarse-textured dark brown hair in a "waterfall," with the "ducktail" in the back, at that time a radical boy's hair style, which has become one of the trademarks of the 1950's. He was considered shy, quiet, but friendly to anyone who wanted to converse with him. "Everybody knew Ritchie in school," said Manny Sandoval, another Pacoima Junior High schoolmate. "Although he was popular, he wouldn't put you down." One complicating factor concerns how

Ritchie may have fared in regards to race relations. His fair complexion may have been somewhat advantageous in respect to some Anglos and certainly later on when he became nationally popular, but not always in respect to those of his own background. A colloquial term for a light-skinned Mexican, not necessarily derogatory, is *güero*, which was probably used toward Ritchie. A more derogatory term, *falso*, regardless of color, was also used. "A lot of people used to laugh at us and put us down [for singing]," said Sandoval. "They used to put Ritchie down, especially the Mexican kids. They used to call him *falso* and call me that, too, because we liked to be with everybody—Blacks, Mexicans, whites, whatever. So they [Chicanos] wouldn't come around that much to group into the music thing with us. It would be the Blacks, some of the whites and a few Chicanos." Tovar also recalled that the majority of people who got together with Ritchie were from the same neighborhood. Despite what others may have thought of him, most of Ritchie's friends were Chicanos or Blacks. His friendships with whites (outside of a few like Chaubet) came much later through his musical exposure at private parties in high school and with the Silhouettes. Also, Ritchie did not go out much with girls, although Sandoval remembered Ritchie occasionally going with a girl named "Nancy." There may have been a weight problem, though Ritchie did draw a considerable female crowd at the sessions. Describing these jam sessions, Sandoval said, "There weren't that many musicians in the school, just Ritchie and a guy who called himself 'Tony Casanova,' but whose real name was Jutilio Pérez. Both would bring their guitars and we'd all get together to sing. The ones who would sing would be the Blacks, Ritchie and Tony, me, my cousin Bob Cano. Not too many of the whites would sing. They would just watch and clap, stuff like that. The Mexican kids would kind of be in the background. This was the thing."

Jutilio Pérez, a.k.a., "Tony Casanova," was somewhat the opposite of Ritchie—aggressive, often wearing brighter and bolder clothes, and usually imitating the gyrations and style of Elvis Presley. He was put down as well, if not more so than Ritchie, for his extrinsic behavior. Many thought it would be Jutilio rather than Ritchie who would eventually "make it."

Sandoval remembered singing mostly rhythm and blues and rock and roll at the group sessions. "About the only Mexican song we sang was 'La Bamba,'" he said. "Ritchie taught me the riffs. That was the first thing I ever learned how to play on the guitar. That was the closest thing we sang in Spanish, though I'm sure he knew others."

Probably the most curious and unprecedented experience that developed at Pacoima Junior High centering around Ritchie was the creation of a game song called "Mama Long." This game song seemed to center around Ritchie's talents and the ensuing result depended upon group participation as well as Ritchie's presence. Sandoval vividly described it:

"'Mama Long' was a group song and anybody could sing it if they had a verse they had made up. Ritchie would start playing, some would start harmonizing the name 'Mama Long,' getting into the rhythm in all different ways, 'cause you wouldn't sing the song the same way all the time. Either the singing line would be different or the rhythm would sometimes change. It depended on how and what type of rhythm you got going." He gave a couple of examples of how a line in a verse would go:

> MAMA LONG, is her name
> Making love is her game
> Oh, MAMA LONG, MAMA LONG . . .
>
> or
>
> Oh, MAMA LONG, she's so fine
> Makes all the guys stand in line,
> Oh, MAMA LONG, etc.
>
> All the guys just can't wait
> To see if they could get a date
> With MAMA LONG, MAMA LONG, etc.

"We used to mention various dances in the song, too," said Sandoval. He named some of those dances popular in the L.A. area at the time: the *choke*, a couple dance like the swing which was done with handkerchiefs; the *shuffle*, a couple slow dance. There was also a dance step called the *bee-bop*. Ironically, this step was performed by Gilbert Melgar who played the role of Ritchie Valens in the movie "The Buddy Holly Story." Possibly, this step may have been a precursor to the *mash potatoes*, a dance from the early 60's that Sandoval called a "refined bee-bop."

He said, "If we couldn't think of any more words, the guys would just fade out with 'Mama Long, Mama Long' like the record." Sandoval could not recall the origin of the game song's name. He vaguely remembered a song called "Mama Love" which may have been connected to the commercially popular song "Honey Love," made famous by Clyde McPhatter and the Drifters. He also said, "Very possibly, 'Mama Long' was somehow at first dirty. When there weren't any girls around, the words would get a little risqué." In giving credit to the song, he added, "It was something we remembered we used to do with Ritchie and that was one of the things. The two Black guys harmonizing were very important in this. Without them, it would be just Ritchie singing." Another song Sandoval remembered singing with Ritchie was the Fats Domino classic "Going Down to the River," which they sang as a duo. Ritchie also sang solo a variety of songs by Little Richard and Larry Williams, the Everly Brothers and Elvis. The concept of changing the melody and rhythm in the game song "Mama Long" was to figure strongly in Ritchie's music henceforth. Brandt summarized it as such: "Some people thought Ritchie had become famous too easily. But you have to have an art, a gift in music to be really successful. He was new, a different kind of singer."

*   *   *

Five months prior to Ritchie's graduation in 1957, tragedy struck Pacoima Junior High School. On the morning of January 31, 1957, while the winter graduates were practicing their speeches in the auditorium for graduation on the following day, a transport F-89J jet collided with a navy plane over Las Tunas Canyon. The transport plane exploded over Pacoima Junior High and the wreckage was scattered all over the athletic field. Eight people were killed—the crew and three schoolchildren—and ninety people were injured. Schwartz continues to give lectures to this day on how to prepare for such school disasters. This tragedy led to the construction of Pacoima Memorial Lutheran Hospital, for at the time of the accident the nearest hospital facilities were in San Fernando. Said Brandt, "I felt that I was marred for about five years afterward emotionally and some of my students had to be hospitalized permanently. Nobody got out of it without being scarred a little bit."

Apparently, Ritchie was also "scarred" by this incident, even though he had been away from school that day. He was attending the funeral of his grandfather, Frank Reyes. The Reyes as well as his mother asserted Ritchie's fear of planes. Ernestine

Reyes explained: "He was leery about airplanes because living here in Pacoima he'd seen all these little airplanes coming down real close to the roads. He once said, 'It's bad enough flying in the big ones, let alone the little ones.'" Eliodoro (or Lelo as he prefers to be called) Reyes recalled what he said to his nephew when they were driving down San Fernando Road one day: "I said, 'Don't ever get on that silly little stupid thing that crawls by itself,' and Ritchie said, 'I'll never get on one of those.'"

The 9th-grade graduating class individual photos in the Pacoima Junior High School *Torch*, 1956-57. Ritchie was about 15 years old. Photo: S. Guitarez/B. Mendheim collection.

Group photo of the graduating class at Pacoima Junior High School, Spring 1957. Ritchie is wearing the then-popular "waterfall" hairstyle. Photo: S. Guitarez/B. Mendheim collection.

Ritchie posed for this touristy shot, probably taken sometime in 1957, during a visit to Tijuana with his aunt and uncle, Ernestine and Lelo Reyes (right), and two other relatives. Photo: Ernestine Reyes collection.

Ritchie and some of the members of the Silhouettes. Standing, left to right: Ray Lerma, Walter Préndez, Dave Torreta, Conrad Jones, Walter Takaki, Ritchie. Sitting, l. to r.: Armando "Lefty" Ortiz, Gil Rocha, Frankie Gallardo. Photo was taken at American Legion Hall in San Fernando, possibly in Autumn 1957. Gil Rocha collection.

Ritchie performing with the Silhouettes. Ray Lerma (left) and Gil Rocha (right, on vibraphones). American Legion Hall, San Fernando (1957?). Photo: Gil Rocha collection.

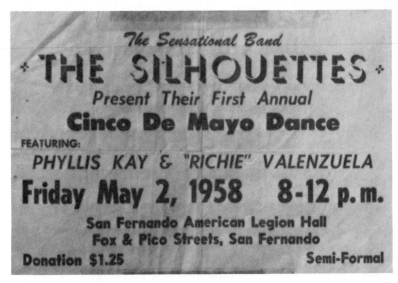

Flyer announcing the Silhouettes' dance, with Ritchie as one of the featured performers. Photo: S. Guitarez/Ernestine Reyes collection.

Ritchie with teenage reporters from various high schools in the Los Angeles area at radio station KFWB (L.A.). The photo may have been taken on Oct. 11, 1958. Ritchie is upper row, right, and DJ Ernie Fields is upper row, center. Photo: Tom Powell collection. (Powell is in the photo, seated, with glasses.)

Ritchie with high school reporters at the KFWB radio interview (Oct. 11, 1958?) in Los Angeles. Photo: Tom Powell collection.

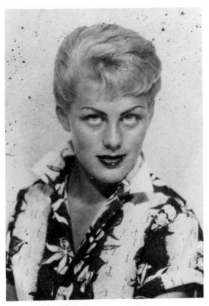

Photo of Donna Ludwig (Fox), taken around 1958, for whom the song "Donna" was written. Photo: Jerry Faulkner collection.

Ted Quillin, DJ of KFWB radio, Los Angeles, a confidant of Ritchie's. Photo: Ernestine Reyes collection.

Ritchie performing at San Fernando High School, Autumn (?) 1958. Photo from the San Fernando High School yearbook, 1959. B. Mendheim collection.

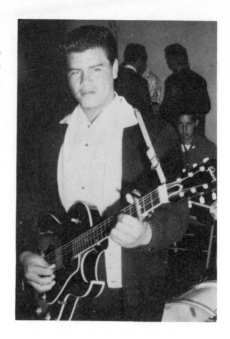

Ritchie performing at Gail Smith's Halloween party, San Fernando, CA, Oct. 31, 1958. Smith (now González) is second from the left; also seen are Judy (in center) and John (behind Ritchie) of "John & Judy." Photo: Gerd Muesfeldt collection.

Ritchie performing at the Pacoima Junior High School concert, which was released on the album "Ritchie Valens in Concert at Pacoima Junior High." Don Phillips on drums. Photo: Gerd Muesfeldt collection.

The Pacoima Junior High auditorium, where Ritchie performed on December 10, 1958. Photo: B. Mendheim.

Ritchie backstage at the Alan Freed
Christmas Show, Loew's State Theater,
New York City, late December (?) 1958.
Photo: B. Mendheim.

Ritchie with Diane Olsen, backstage at
the Alan Freed Christmas Show, December 1958. Photo: Ernestine Reyes collection.

3

"LITTLE RICHARD OF THE SAN FERNANDO VALLEY"

Performances at Private Parties

From 1955 through 1958, Ritchie played at many private parties throughout the San Fernando Valley before and during his association with the Silhouettes. They were chances for exposure and for an occasional dollar sorely needed. According to Tovar, Ritchie was always on call for a party. Tovar said, "We would meet at different houses and have a jam session."

John ("Big John") Alcaraz, an older acquaintance of Ritchie's, remembered that many of these parties took place in Pacoima, San Fernando, Granada Hills, Sylmar, and other areas of the northern Valley. "Ritchie was going to junior high when we were going to high school," said Alcaraz. "He didn't hang around too many people his own age.

"He used to do mostly Little Richard. He'd also sing 'Come On, Let's Go,' and the Everly Brothers' 'Wake Up, Little Suzie.'"

Louis "Skip" Raring, who lived a few blocks from Ritchie and also attended San Fernando High, was also older than Ritchie. He recalled that during the late 50's, there were car clubs that were mostly either all-Anglo or all-Chicano. The largest of the Anglo ones were the Igniters, the Drifters, and the Lost Angels. The largest Chicano gang was the Lobos. "They were called 'car clubs' but essentially they were just gangs," said Raring, who was a member of the Lost Angels. His club and the other Anglo clubs were big on giving private parties, but Raring was a close friend of Ritchie's. Ritchie used to come over to his house to listen to his record collection. Raring's father also had an elaborate hi-fi set and amplifiers so Ritchie liked to set up his electric guitar and play. "We had a special music room in my house," said Raring.

"There were speakers all over the place. Ritchie used to listen to the music, then he'd sing. From what I remember, Ritchie never had a record player. That's why we never went to his house."

Raring described how Ritchie got involved with singing for the Anglo car clubs: "After I had known Ritchie for a month or so, I brought it up in one of the club meetings that there was this fantastic guy we called 'Little Ritchie.' I told them about Ritchie but at first they weren't very excited because he was a Mexican guy. Anyway, he started singing at our parties. Everyone just loved him and he loved it. It was a first time for him. He had sung at little things at Pacoima Junior High, but we were a big club and our parties had a lot of people. When he sang, everyone really got into him, clapping and just going crazy. They never heard anything like him before. Ritchie got so wrapped up in these parties that he used to call me every day and say, 'Hey, Skip! When's the next pah-ty?' He used to call it '*pah*-ty.' Even if it was something at the spur of the moment, we'd call him up. He couldn't wait to go. He must've sung at fifteen or twenty of our parties. I don't know what we used to raise, but we took up a little collection for him by passing the hat."

Little Richard's songs had considerable influence on Ritchie's music and Raring described what he remembered about it: "It was just a medium to start a song. 'Jenny, Jenny, Jenny' was Ritchie's favorite [Little Richard] song. He would start singing it, keeping the chords going, then a minute later, he'd make up his own words and he'd be off on his own. It was no longer Little Richard coming out. It was different! He would do that with other songs (not necessarily Little Richard), for instance, 'Sweet Little Sixteen,' playing the guitar like Chuck Berry. The first couple of seconds would be just that, then he'd start making up his own words and telling his own story. That was pure Ritchie, which never really came out in his [commercial] recordings."

Raring also recalled a more negative side to the parties. Occasionally, a fight would break out or some people would even smoke marijuana which used to turn Ritchie off. There was some friction between Raring and Ritchie on this point. "Because I was older," said Raring, "Ritchie used to look up to me. Then when he saw the kind of people I used to run around with, he was very disappointed with me." At these parties people also drank, although the majority of them were under twenty-one. The concern about teenagers drinking was not as extensive then as it is now. Ritchie did drink but not in excess, according to Raring, Tovar and Alcaraz. But the marijuana issue came to a head and became Raring's last encounter with Ritchie. Said Raring, "The last time I saw Ritchie was right after he had signed a contract, though he did not make a record yet (1958). I was going through a rough period in my life. Ritchie had just moved and this time he had me come over to his house when he was recording something and wanted me to hear it. (Note: this may have occurred at the Reyes' home where Ritchie also stayed. The Reyes did not recall the event, so it may have happened when they were not home.) I went and brought some of my friends and he started singing to us. They pulled out some joints and started lighting them up. This *really* bothered him. He gave me a look as if he couldn't believe it. That was the way he was, so I never heard from him again. Of course, he was gone all the time, too, but some of my friends would see him from time to time and he would ask, 'How's Skip?'"

Summing up his feelings about Ritchie, Raring added, "He was a man for all seasons. He never appeared to be conscious of the difference between Mexican, Black and white. There was something different about him. He loved life and always had a smile when I saw him."

The Silhouettes

Sometime around October, 1957, shortly after he entered San Fernando High School as a sophomore, Ritchie began to perform with a group of other musicians, some of whom were friends since childhood. After Ritchie's death, magazine writers erroneously stated that Ritchie founded this group called the Silhouettes. However, the question of who was the actual leader of the band remains unresolved to this day, even among the former members, though all attest that Ritchie was never the "founder" of the group. The two major people involved with forming the group were Gilbert Rocha and William Jones, whose stories about how the group was formed differ widely.

According to Gil Rocha, a professional vibes player, the forming of the Silhouettes began this way:

"I was twenty-one and the others were in school. I was getting this band together and Conrad Jones, the drummer, told me of a kid in school that played guitar pretty good. I didn't want a guitar but I wanted to hear him anyway. That night, there was a knock on the door and when I opened it, there was this little kid, guitar in hand with a little amp. He didn't look Mexican to me and I said to myself, 'Who's this little Okie?' Not that I was prejudiced, but I wanted to keep the band mostly Mexican. [Ritchie] struck me as quiet and shy. He looked older so I offered him a drink which he accepted. The only drink in the house was a half bottle of tequila and we sat there and drank it. I later found out that he was sick for the next two days. Ritchie later told me that he did not drink but he didn't want to say no to me.

"In the beginning, I had the Silhouettes. It was my decision to let Ritchie in the band. We started out as a quintet: myself, vibes; Ritchie, guitar; Conrad ('Nino') Jones, drums; Frank Gallardo, piano; and Walter Takaki, sax. We didn't have a name until there was a record that came out ('Silhouettes' by the Rays, which was released October, 1957). We started using that name. The guys wanted more instruments so we started adding a couple of trumpets and Conrad's brother, Bill, came in as a sax player in January [1958].

"To get started, I rented the American Legion Hall under my name. We used to have dances for about twenty-five or thirty cents! About the fifth one, we were getting more popular and did dances for social clubs."

Rocha has a record of the dances he promoted from October 19, 1957, to May 2, 1958. According to this record, the first big dance was a Lost Angels anniversary party (which Raring vividly remembers ending up with a fight between the Angels and the Lobos), which took place at the Union Hall in Panorama City. The last dance was a "Cinco de Mayo" dance at the American Legion Hall in San Fernando. After the "Cinco de Mayo" dance, Rocha left the Silhouettes, because, as he explained: "The boys were jealous that I was their leader. I can see why now years later—they were in school together and in the spotlight of most of the band's fans. People would see them in school and naturally would ask who was the leader. We were the only band in town then so the boys really got big-headed. Another point: As in any band, the *money* thing came up and I was accused of skimming off the top of the take at the door. One member started that rumor. It was totally untrue and the only one who stuck up for me was Ritchie. He also said, 'It's your band. You started it. You tell them you're the leader.' He was always on my side."

William (Bill) Jones, a retired Marine officer, had a different story:

"Basically, Gil started an original group that had himself on the vibes, Conrad/Nino on the drums, Ritchie, the guitar player, Frankie as the piano player and Walter [Takaki] playing tenor sax. On the second gig, I played alto and tenor sax, and clarinet. Walter, Nino and Richard [Ritchie] asked me to play because they needed some more depth. At the end of that night, there was a big flail. Gil had a song he was trying to push. The guys were trying to tell him he had no voice, to drop the song. Gil said that if we're not going to push it, he'll quit the group and we said that was fine to quit. Number two: The group was pretty rattled up because after the first gig, Gil would take them into the bedroom and pay them off. He would pay each one on a different scale and cautioned them not to tell the other guys. That's not the way to run a band.

"The name 'Silhouettes' was *my* brainstorm. I contracted for a gig at the Sportsman's Lodge in Hollywood one night and they asked what name to put down. I pulled 'The Silhouettes' out of the air. That's how we got stuck with it. Ritchie was with me and Don Phillips who replaced Nino when he got drafted. Gil did not promote any of the Silhouettes' dances. Once he left the group, that is, *his* group, he had nothing to do with the Silhouettes or with Ritchie getting his break."

There also is an apparent disagreement on who the actual members of the Silhouettes were and what they played or sang. Basically, the breakdown was the following:

Gil Rocha	vibes
Richard Valenzuela	electric guitar/vocalist
Frankie Gallardo	piano
Conrad "Nino" Jones	drums (replaced by Don Phillips)
Walter Takaki	saxophone
Bill Jones	saxophone
Ray Lerma	saxophone
Dave Torreta	trumpet
Armando "Lefty" Ortiz	trumpet
Freddie Aguilera	trumpet
Walter Préndez	vocalist
Phyllis Kay (Romano)	vocalist
Rubén Herrera	alto sax
Sal Barragán	alto sax

| Augie Gauthrie | congas (not in Rocha's documents) |
| Emma Franco | vocalist (not in Rocha's documents) |

Walter Préndez, whom Jones stated "was not a regular member and never paid by me," wrote: "I was a bona-fide member of the band and I got paid after each and every dance. Ritchie and I sang duos [a photo exists of the two singing together] and I did some solos. 'We Belong Together' was a very requested song (originally recorded by a duo, Robert and Johnny). Sometimes, I did the lead, other times, Ritchie did the lead. I sang rhythm and blues and some standards that were around then. Ritchie sang everything that was asked of him and he did it well."

Other members of the Silhouettes were split between Rocha's and Jones' claims. Walter Takaki could not remember who founded and named the group, but he tended to be more in agreement with Rocha. Takaki stated, "Gil said the first job we played, we got thirty-five dollars. The first job we played, we got nothing! People walked out on us. That's how bad we were. That was our first job."

Armando "Lefty" Ortiz recalled that Rocha founded and named the group the Silhouettes and was with the group for almost a year ('57 to '58). But Ortiz added that Jones was "the brains that kept us together."

Frankie Gallardo said that Rocha was there at the beginning but Ritchie had more doings with Bill Jones and Rocha only stayed with the group a very short time. Said Gallardo, "The story of Ritchie meeting Gil in which he knocked at Gil's door is not true. I would say that Gil actually met Ritchie through the Joneses. Richard was already playing solo but he wanted to play with the group. We started off with piano [myself] and drums [Conrad]. Then we had a guitar [Ritchie]. Gil came along and said, 'I'm starting this band.' It took a while before we even really considered his offer. He came out with this idea that he already had a big band before. Being young, fifteen to sixteen, we thought that maybe this guy has played around. But then we found out he didn't have that experience he told us. He just stuck around, didn't do too much playing. He told us he used to play vibraphones. When we went to Gil's house, he didn't have one. I don't think he even played until a little bit later.

"We helped him a lot and he knew a lot of people, so he got us a few jobs. Then Bill [Jones] took over. He got us more jobs than Gil. Bill became sort of the manager. That's why there's that little friction. Gil was our manager, too, but I don't remember Gil doing enough like Bill did. Bill took over all the bookings and we did real well with him. We all got together and decided on the name, 'The Silhouettes.'"

Préndez not only contended that Rocha did promote some of the dances, but also that Ritchie's mother promoted a few. He said, "I might add that Ritchie did a lot of playing on his own to help his mom out with the money."

Freddy Aguilera had this to say about the controversy:

"Lefty [Ortiz] asked me if I wanted to play with the band and I said yeh. I was turning seventeen. That's when I met Ritchie. We used to practice at Gil's house. Ritchie and I became very good friends. We were *all* good friends, I mean, Jesus! That's why I don't understand why Bill and Gil are having their problems. Bill or Gil would take care of the business. If I'm not mistaken, both of them had a part in managing the Silhouettes. Both of them *should* take the credit. I don't think it should be just one of them."

The dates Rocha documented are widely enough spaced to allow for other functions for the Silhouettes. Perhaps, Jones may have been the impetus behind the undocumented events as well as those which occurred after Rocha left the band.

Practice sessions took place in the individual members' homes, especially Rocha's, Takaki's and the Joneses'. Ortiz remembered that the father of the Joneses gave the group some musical coaching. Bill Jones confirmed this: "My dad was a musician for thirty-seven years and he gave us a hand. There was also another retired musician in Pacoima [whose name he could not recall] who gave us pointers, because when we first started, we were mediocre. I taped the group on their third gig and they just didn't have it."

According to Jones, Ritchie was *not* the key singer in the Silhouettes, though he had some "good innate talent." Even after Ritchie cut "Come On, Let's Go," he was still not the featured Silhouettes' singer, but a woman named Emma Franco was. Jones agreed that Phyllis Kay (a.k.a. Romano) sang with the group but he attested, "I never billed Phyllis and Ritchie together. That was one of the reasons she quit the band and was replaced by Emma Franco." He was referring to a poster for a Silhouettes dance that featured "Phyllis Kay and Richie Valenzuela" which he called "a fake, plain and simple."

However, Rocha asserted that Ritchie was the featured singer, because, as he said, "Ritchie was my front center. Later, Préndez carried two numbers, Kay, two, and Ritchie did the rest. It was mostly early rock and roll and rhythm and blues stuff. Ritchie didn't sing any original songs 'cause as the leader, I picked out the music for the group."

But Aguilera disagreed: "Ritchie did a lot of his [original] stuff at the Silhouettes' functions. I know he did because at practice, he used to say, 'Look, I'm gonna try this,' and he sang some of his songs for the dances."

All the former Silhouettes agreed that Ritchie sang mostly Little Richard and other current music of the period, but there were some conflicting opinions about whether Latin music was performed. Ortiz, Gallardo and Aguilera all remembered doing Latin music. Said Aguilera, "In those days, there were a lot of *corridos* (traditional Mexican folk ballads, often using contemporary themes and performed as a popular medium). We were one of the first bands [in the Valley] to break into *corridos*." He added that Ritchie did not sing much in Spanish "because [they] didn't think his Spanish was that hot. But Ritchie would use the *grito* (traditional musical cry) in doing 'La Bamba.'" Gallardo also admitted to doing popular Latin music, especially at wedding receptions and other occasion dances. "I was the one who did most of the selections of that music," said Gallardo.

But Bill Jones remarked: "Ritchie did not sing Latin songs. None whatsoever. 'La Bamba,' which Richard did not like to do, was my doing. We needed a cha-cha at a gig one night, the crowd wanted more Latin. We were hurting and I said we'd do 'La Bamba,' and Richard said, 'I don't like it,' and I said, 'Tough! I'm running it and we're gonna do it!' and Richard said, 'Okay.' Nino was on timbales and drums, Richard on guitar, Frank on the piano and we just riffed it for about ten minutes. From then on, it was a standard for us."

According to Rocha, Ritchie did know and sing Latin music, but the majority of the band could not back him up. Despite Rocha's initial attempts to keep the band "mostly Mexican," it was definitely a multi-ethnic band consisting of Chicanos, Blacks (the Joneses), one Japanese (Takaki) and Italians (Torreta, Barragán). Said Rocha, "Once, we did a free thing and nobody showed up but me, Ritchie and Walter Takaki. We couldn't do anything about the band, so Ritchie just carried the whole show that night and he sang all those Mexican *corridos*."

Regardless of how important Ritchie's role in the group may have been, his showmanship made an impression on other members of the Silhouettes. Both Takaki and Aguilera recalled that Ritchie never danced and played guitar at the same time, but would often get down on his knees while playing the guitar. "He wouldn't go crazy like Elvis," said Aguilera, "but he would get the people moving, reacting. He had a lot of charisma. People would start moving as soon as he started playing." "He went by what the crowd felt," said Takaki. Gallardo added, "It would depend on the kind of mood he was in. Sometimes, he would sit down on the edge of the stage and just sing. Ritchie never sang without his guitar [except for duos with Préndez]. 'Framed' was a special solo for him. He would even change the melody, making it longer or shorter."

Lillian Beckett, Rocha's sister, commented that Ritchie had a special charisma felt by the female crowd at dances. When on stage, he would flirt back at a screaming, clapping crowd of girls. "That was when he was behind that guitar," said Beckett. "He had a twinkle in his eye and he used to kind of wink in a shy way. But when I first met Ritchie, he was *so* shy, it was unbelievable! And he didn't really talk to any other girls. The girls would approach him. I just about went to every dance and I can really honestly say that Ritchie never took a girl to the dances." Préndez also agreed: "Ritchie never took a girl to one of our dances but he did talk to a lot of them at the dances."

Besides the Legion Halls in San Fernando (located on Fox and Pico Sts.) and Pacoima (now called Valdez' Dance Hall on Van Nuys Blvd.), the Silhouettes played at the Carpenter's Hall in Van Nuys, San Fernando Recreation Park, Pacoima Recreation Park, and San Fernando High School. The "gigs" were almost strictly in the San Fernando Valley area, except for one dance in Los Angeles (documented by Rocha) and a dance, according to Jones, given at the Sportsman's Lodge in Hollywood in honor of Bud Abbott's and Louis Costello's nieces.

The pay was relatively low for the band but a member could on occasion receive up to eighteen or twenty dollars a night. Former members recalled some good times together with Rit-

chie. Said, Aguilera, "We'd have some house parties especially at
the Joneses' home. We would get our instruments out and start
playing, messing around. We'd really have real nice parties . . .
our kick was 'Silver Satin,' (a kind of brandy or fruit liquor) to
calm our nerves before a performance. We never used any pot.
The heaviest we ever got was some uppers, just whites."

Gallardo disagreed on the use of pills or "whites" but admitted that they did drink often. Concerning Ritchie he said,
"He'd take a shot, not to get drunk, before a performance, just to
get in the mood and relax."

As a member of the Silhouettes, Ritchie's personality remained about the same as it had been in junior high. He continued to get along with everybody, within the group and outside of
the group. "Ritchie actually got the two gangs, the Lobos and the
Angels, a little bit closer together," said Takaki. "Whenever he
was playing, they would get along just fine." Once, Takaki remembered that the group had to stop Ritchie from getting into a
fight at a dance, but for the most part Ritchie was rarely hot-
tempered. "There were times when he used to cuss up a storm,"
said Aguilera, "if something [musically] didn't come out right
when he was playing. After that, he'd be all right. It was just the
normal thing for him." Gallardo did not remember Ritchie arguing about anything: "He would make all these facial expressions showing his likes and dislikes but other than that, he never
made a big scene about anything. For instance, he'd look directly
at a person and keep looking while cleaning his guitar, with one
eye opened." Also, Ritchie liked to use the musicians' jargon of
the day, especially the word "cool." "He was hardly in any trouble," said Aguilera. "The only trouble we got in was that him and
I would get sick from that damn wine (Silver Satin) and the older
guys would take care of us then."

Up to the time of his first recording, Ritchie was still playing
with the Silhouettes. The obligations demanded from both
sources were sometimes conflicting. Ritchie never formally split
from the group, though he played less with them once he was
established as a solo act. "When we'd ask him about a gig," said
Aguilera, "he would say he had to be doing something else. It was
getting to his head. Then later, after 'American Bandstand,' it
really went to his head! But he had a reason. It was very difficult
in those days to be somebody. He was a good musician and it was
hard for Chicanos at that time. I even remember taking a friend

of mine out to dinner here in Pacoima and they refused us service! So you can see how rough it was at the time. You have to give Ritchie a lot of credit." Aguilera best expressed his feelings on some of the splintering that resulted within the Silhouettes over Ritchie Valens' fame: "To me, they are acting like children. They forget about Ritchie. The more you dig into it, the more you'll find, 'I did this and I did that,' and that's impossible. If they were here now, I would tell them to get it together."

Into High School and Into the Big Time

Besides the occasional concerts with or without the Silhouettes, Ritchie's experiences at San Fernando High were rather minimal. He was there in school for approximately one year and then stopped, probably around late October, 1958, when his recordings became successful and he was obliged to travel. Very few teachers at the high school remembered who Ritchie was. His school activities were limited to playing for high school dances and assemblies. According to the former music teacher, Ritchie was virtually uninvolved with any high school functions in music such as choir, musicals, pageants, etc. However, a photo does exist of him performing at a high school talent show known as the "Fernando Follies."

Once he became popular, San Fernando's school paper, *The Whirlwind*, did a special article on Ritchie, which appeared on October 19, 1958. This article is assumed to be an interview in which Ritchie expressed a "desire to study music into the college level." It was also at San Fernando High that Ritchie became more acquainted with a sophomore who later inspired the song "Donna." Donna Ludwig (now Fox) first met Ritchie at an Igniters' party when he was playing with the Silhouettes. She said, "Before I left the party, he asked me for my phone number but nothing came of it as I had been seeing this other fellow. The next time I saw Ritchie, I ran into him in the corridors at San Fernando High and said, 'Hi, Ritchie!' and he said, 'Well, I'll be damned! Hi, blondie!' We would walk in the corridors in school all the time and he would meet me outside. The school would have noon-time dances and I would dance with him. He was always so sweet and treated me so nice. My father didn't care too much for him, so I really wasn't allowed to date him. But I'd meet him at roller skating rinks and parties on the side. We became quite close."

Fox had vivid memories of the assemblies Ritchie performed in at high school: "He would love to get those assemblies rocking. He did a lot of Little Richard's stuff, which never came out in the Del-Fi recordings. One of his favorite numbers was 'The Girl Can't Help It.' He also performed 'Boney-Maronie' (recorded by Larry Williams). He would just tear up that assembly. They would holler and scream, jump up and down; I remember one assembly they wouldn't let him out! He had to keep on playing. The principal tried to call the assembly over and the kids wouldn't leave!"

Donna went to James Monroe High School shortly after Ritchie left San Fernando High. Ritchie was a junior at the time and was supposed to have a tutor while on the road. Said Fox: "I don't know if Keane ever got him that tutor because he was legally under age. They were passing him off as eighteen."

Two years earlier, in December, 1956, Ritchie's family had been forced to leave the property of his deceased father, unable to keep up the increased payments. They moved to a squat little house in Pacoima located at 13327 Gain St., which is no longer there. Donna remembered it as a "terrible little house." Around this time, Ritchie's mother had another baby, Mario, in addition to her two daughters and two sons. Connie was subsisting on a pension of one hundred and forty dollars a month left by Joseph Steve, as well as what she could make by taking an occasional job as a waitress. Sometime around 1957, Robert married and lived separately which somewhat alleviated the overcrowded home. But the financial needs of the family were pressing enough for Ritchie to be obliged at his early age to lend some support to his mother. He had a devotional love for his mother and most everyone remembered Ritchie always speaking well of her. He felt first and foremost the need to do something about lessening the financial strain on his family. But with a new baby in the house, it made it rather difficult for Ritchie to practice his music as often as he should. Since his aunt and uncle, the Reyes, did not have children at the time, they had the extra space. They had recently married and purchased a home with extra rooms. Ernestine stated: "He came often and stayed with us. In the first place, Connie had no money and Ritchie needed this and that, so Lelo was the only one who could help him out. So Ritchie decided to stay with us. He was still going to school and the only money he got was with the band and that hardly wasn't anything! That kid, poor thing, didn't even have a shirt to take a picture in! Ritchie had to borrow all of Lelo's clothes. Connie just couldn't afford to give him the stuff to get him started."

In January, 1958, the sixty-five-dollar mortgage payment came due on the Gain Street house. It had been common for Connie to occasionally rent out the Pacoima Legion Hall for her son to have parties and raise money for expenses. Ritchie decided to throw a dance at the hall that month to pay for the taxes on the house. He and his mother rented the Legion Hall for a "mere" fifty-seven dollars, which included a cop and a janitor. The Silhouettes also participated. The dance cost one dollar and twenty-five cents stag, two dollars a couple. They made one hundred and twenty-five dollars in the process. Said Chaubet who remembered that particular dance: "Since Ritchie was already known at school he had a helluva turnout that night. That's when Bob Keane discovered him right there."

Keane did not attend the function but a fellow who represented him did. It was he who actually got Ritchie on his way.

4

THE DEL-FI SESSIONS

Doug Macchia, a former graduate of San Fernando High School, was already twenty years old when Ritchie started going to school there. Macchia had a partnership in printing and advertising work and as a result met Bob Keane, who was starting a record company. Keane was searching for talent who were very much into rock and roll and Macchia agreed to get some people together on tape for him. As Macchia recalled it: "Through various friends I found out about Ritchie. It turned out that Gil and I went to school together, as did some other friends of mine, Bill and Conrad Jones. I went down to the American Legion Hall in San Fernando and taped the Silhouettes and taped Ritchie and a couple of other people at the same time. I also went around and taped other people in different places, then took the tape to Bob [Keane]. Of all the people I had taped, Bob thought Ritchie was the best. I went back to Ritchie and told him that Bob was interested in having him come back for an audition. My recollection is that we had it set for a Saturday morning because Ritchie was going to school."

Macchia did not remember exactly when the auditions occurred; however, there is some speculation as to the month. Several 1959 fan magazines stated that Ritchie auditioned for Keane on his birthday, May 13th, "just for luck," as one of the articles put it. This seemed highly unlikely because May 13th was on a Tuesday. No one else has any recollections of the exact date of the audition, but speculation dictates that it may have occurred either on May 10th or May 17th, the two Saturdays fairly close to Ritchie's birthday.

Macchia recounted what happened that Saturday:

"I went to pick up Ritchie and when I picked him up, he wasn't at home (Macchia could not remember if Ritchie was at the Reyes home). We went back to Ritchie's house because he was going to have to watch the kids. His mother had to go to an uncle or somebody to borrow money for the rent, but that wasn't my feeling after talking to him. He didn't want to go to the audition. As a matter of fact, he absolutely wasn't going to go! He was just plain scared.

"At the time, Ritchie was putting the finishing touches on 'Donna,' as we were waiting for his mother to get back. As I recall, I helped him write two or three lines, but I don't recall which ones they were. He had changed the name several times— I couldn't recall which names they were—but that morning, he decided to name the song 'Donna,' because he had just broken up with a girl by that name and he was writing it for her to get her back. It was about two hours that we sat there talking and I was trying to calm him down, trying to get him to go to the audition. I finally got him to go but he wanted to go with some of his buddies and I said, 'No. You come with me,' because I wanted to be sure that he got there. But as I recall, some of the guys [from the Silhouettes] did come to the audition at Keane's home, because the cops came by. They tried to bust them because they were mostly Mexican and it was an all-Anglo neighborhood, up in the Hollywood Hills. The cops tried to get them out of the car and might have searched them, I don't remember, but Ritchie was inside Keane's home at the time. I came out and talked to the police and they went away very suspiciously. It was about 10 A.M. or noon.

"In the basement, which I didn't know at the time, Keane had a complete recording setup. It was very elaborate and expensive, like a studio one. He had a drummer with him who was the backup drummer for Ricky Nelson (Earl Palmer). There were also one or two other professional musicians who were backup men. I didn't know they were going to be there. Keane had a full 8-track setup which wasn't for demos only. They were to be cut and produced!

"When Ritchie went in, he was so nervous. They had to take the musicians out of the room, because with the musicians, he was not too good at first. But he finally calmed down and the kid was just incredible. I mean, he just really got into the music and forgot everybody was there and everybody really got enthused. He really got hot. We were there, probably four to six hours."

One song, "Rock Little Donna," the name given to a demo

recording of "That's My Little Suzie," which in later years was released on an album unaffiliated with Del-Fi, Macchia recognized as the first song Ritchie did for Keane in his basement studio. "He did that song two or three times, just the guitar and him," he said. "I also remembered that he did 'Donna' and 'La Bamba.'" Macchia could not recall the names of the other songs auditioned, but he suspects that most of the songs recorded then went onto Ritchie's albums. In addition, Keane kept the tape of the Silhouettes Macchia did at the dance.

Bill Jones, who attended Ritchie's audition, also had a story to tell of it:

"When Doug [Macchia] came to the American Legion Hall, Gil had long been detached from the band. Doug told me he knew of a recording studio that was looking for some new talent and I said he should bring his recorder down since we were playing that Saturday night. So he did and cut a couple of sides of the groups playing and he took that down to Keane. Then he came back and said that Bob would like to see us, specifically the guitar player [Ritchie] who sounded pretty good to him, whereas the rest of the band sounded run-of-the-mill, which we knew. I said it was okay, no problem.

"I put Ritchie in the car, with Nino, and took them down on Westlake, near Echo Park. We set up—Nino on drums, Frank on the piano and Ritchie on the guitar. I was just there with Doug. Bob Keane said to play a few songs and we did. Keane said the kid [Ritchie] sounded pretty good. 'In a Turkish Town' was one of the numbers that they did." Jones also pointed out that he believed the Del-Fi commercial recording of "In a Turkish Town" was actually dubbed over their audition. He said, "Keane made a tape of that which he used later on record."

There were two major people who can claim to be a force behind Ritchie's commercial success: Rene Hall and manager Bob Keane.

Hall, currently of Rene Hall Musical Enterprises in Hollywood, was a close musical associate of Bob Keane. A guitarist by profession, Hall is also an orchestrator, arranger and conductor. He had previously worked with a variety of rhythm and blues and early rock acts, including Specialty recording artists Little Richard, Larry Williams and Sam Cooke. His association with Keane began especially with Cooke, who signed to Keen Records in 1957, of which Bob Keane was partial owner. Said Hall,

"Keane is a former musician, a clarinetist who was fond of Big Band playing, but then got involved with John Simus. With Keen Records, they released a Sam Cooke project which was highly successful. After that, Keane went on his own and created Del-Fi Records. As I recall, Ritchie Valens was his first major hit artist."

Bob Keane (who at the time spelled his name "Keene"), detailed his own background:

"I was sixteen or seventeen years old when I had my own band. I used to play receptions for Duke Ellington, down on Central Avenue, the 'Harlem' of L.A. I was also working with people like Billie Holliday and Lester Young. In 1951, I had a radio show with my own orchestra on NBC. Coming from a jazz background, I don't know how I got into rock and roll. I guess Ritchie's the guy who got me into it because the first record I ever made for my company Del-Fi was a really fine pianist named André Rose. That's how I brought my partner out. I sold Rose's contract to Warner Brothers who were just starting in the recording industry. I produced two of his albums.

"When I got into Ritchie—I really don't know why I even bothered at the moment to do anything with him—it was just one of those things. I was looking around for artists and I figured that this kid's young and he's rock 'n' roll and he's into what's happening. I was operating out of my home and a little Jewish kid [Macchia] was bringing up my [advertising] cards. He asked me if I was interested in hearing a kid out in Pacoima, a really rough part of the San Fernando Valley, whom they called the 'Little Richard of the Valley.'"

Keane did not recall Macchia giving a tape of the Silhouettes to him, nor Ritchie's relationship with the group. He said, "I never heard Ritchie play with anybody but himself, so I don't know much about the Silhouettes," despite several former members remembering Macchia taping their dance for Keane and the accounts of those who attended the audition. Keane recounted the first time he saw Ritchie:

"I saw him at a theater on Saturday morning. He used to get up there in front of the [movie] screen with a little beatup amplifier worth about fifty bucks and his beatup guitar and he'd stand there and sing all these songs. I listened to him and he didn't impress me too much but he had a lot of vitality, a lot of drive, and he had this kind of Latin rock."

In spite of Ritchie's repertoire of Little Richard and current rhythm and blues songs, Keane did not view him in that vein. He told why: "There's no question that everybody in that era was influenced by r 'n' b because it was just coming in. But I don't think it's rhythm and blues unless it's played by a Black man. It's just an influence. The whites can come along or the Chicanos and they can do their interpretation of it but it's not the same."

Bob Keane's Del-Fi records was different in one particular aspect in that it was headed by a *musician*, a phenomenon that rarely occurred on most recording labels. Hall saw Keane as more adventurous in creating different musical ideas than what was currently happening. Keane was the A&R man for his own company. "Having been a musician and a band leader, [Keane] had a thorough knowledge of music as opposed to the average person in the A&R capacity," said Hall. "He was the one who selected the material, had the final say. He was Del-Fi, all by himself, which is something very rare in today's business because most recording executives allocate various responsibilities to different people."

Hall also observed what Keane was trying to promote in Ritchie's music—a "Spanish" rock vein, which had not been promoted well at the time. He was careful in saying that there were *no* Hispanic rock performers around. Ritchie Valens was not the very first rock star of Hispanic heritage, nor of Chicano heritage. A rare r 'n' b song which became a hit around the local area of Los Angeles in 1957 called "Lonely, Lonely Nights" was by Little Julian Herrera, a Chicano. Even Baldemar Huerta, otherwise known as Freddy Fender, recorded "Wasted Days, Wasted Nights," many months before Ritchie recorded "Come On, Let's Go." But the basic difference between these artists and Ritchie Valens was the use of a Latin-tinged sound to a rock and roll beat.

Pérez Prado, who recorded "Patricia" in May, 1958, and had an even earlier hit in February, 1955, with "Cherry Pink and Apple Blossom White," was a Hispanic more in the pop vein. There were also Latin-influenced rock songs sung by Black duos such as Mickey and Sylvia ("Love Is Strange"), and Billie and Lillie ("La Dee Dah") in 1957, or mostly Anglo groups like the Champs with their successful hit, "Tequila," released in early 1958. These artists were non-Latin, as were Valens' sessions musicians, who were mostly Black. Therefore, that "Latin" sound would have to have been supplied by Valens himself. Hall reinforced this belief by saying, "In those days, we were doing a Jan and Dean-type thing for white artists and for Black artists, Sam Cooke, who was different from the majority such as Little Richard, etc. So this style [Valens] was quite a unique situation, this kid. Had he lived, I'm quite sure he would have been a tremendous forerunner in the field of rock music."

Both Hall and drummer Earl Palmer remembered that Saturday morning session at Keane's home and also recalled that former jazz veteran Buddy Clarke played stand-up bass, while Hall played electric guitar and Palmer, drums. Said Hall, "The strangest thing about the biggest hit, 'Donna,' was it was done in the basement of Bob Keane's home on what you would nowadays call a home tape recorder. It was an Ampex, a portable hooked up to high and low impedence imputs, using studio mikes. They did 'Donna' more or less for a demo, but it turned out so good that Keane used it as a [commercial] record. The flip side, 'La Bamba,' was done at a regular recording studio, over at Gold Star. There, we did the [whole] session, including 'La Bamba' and several other tunes that Ritchie Valens had written. They needed a flip side for 'La Bamba' so they just stuck on this 'Oh, Donna' thing we did in the basement."

Stan Ross is the partial owner of Gold Star Recording Studios in Hollywood, which was and still is one of the major recording centers on the West Coast. He remembered Ritchie cutting both "Donna" and "La Bamba," as well as the other songs in one of his major studio rooms. Ross said, "A lot of independent labels didn't have studios. Del-Fi did have a studio but Keane used it for demos and auditions. He didn't have the equipment to do commercial work then, nor the facility to make a commercial recording."

Ross remembered that studio located above Selma and Vine. Del-Fi did have an office there, but a recording studio did not come into being until 1961. On Ritchie's first album, an address is listed as "1610 North Argyle, Hollywood." By the third and last Del-Fi album, *Ritchie Valens in Concert at Pacoima Junior High*, the address is listed as "6277 Selma Avenue, Hollywood." It is doubtful that Ritchie recorded anywhere else than at Keane's basement and Gold Star.

The sessions at Gold Star were done live, according to Ross, except for "Donna" in which there was some overdubbing. "I remember Ritchie in the middle of the room playing guitar while the others played in the background," said Ross. "Ritchie gave it the inspiration by singing live; they got the feel from him. A track would not come off as well. In those days, there wasn't 16- or 24-track. As a matter of fact, there wasn't even 4-track! In '58, it was probably monaural or 2-track. All you did on the 2-track was put the voice on one and the whole band on another. When you hear a stereo today of Ritchie's stuff, it's actually a mono cut reprocessed." Hall also re-emphasized Ross' statement: "The most we had was either a 3- or 4-track machine available and there was very little overdubbing. If I recall, I think everything was done live. We would go into the studio and do the whole thing with the band, with Ritchie singing and playing guitar. Overdubbing wasn't as prolific as it is today with the technological advances of 16- or 24-track machines."

Keane recalled how Ritchie's music was put together:

"Actually, what [Ritchie] did was come to me with a 4- or 8-bar riff, a couple of lines and that's all he ever had: 'I gotta girl, Donna was her name,' and that's all he ever had—'Come on, come on, let's go, let's go,' and that's all there was. On that record I made forty-six edits on tape because he was so out of time. He had no sense of time or anything and we tried to make it fit in. Rene was really fantastic because he would follow [Ritchie], but [Ritchie] was just completely unschooled and unknowledgeable. He knew about three or four chords and everything he wrote was based on these chords. That's why we put other songs like 'Framed,' and 'Bluebirds Over the Mountain' in his first album because we didn't have enough of his songs to go in."

Ross did not feel that Ritchie's music needed as much editing as Keane desired. He explained, "Keane was always into the editing bag. We did a lot of editing on his stuff. Today, you 'punch-in' on multi-track. In those days, you made different takes, five to eight vocal takes, not the music. Once you get past ten, it's '40,' exaggeration time. The tape looks like it's been through World War XIV, because it's spliced so much." Also, Hall had something very different to say about Ritchie's music and how it was put together:

"The music was very well planned in Ritchie's mind. He would sing the melody and he would play the chords on his guitar. Then, he would say what he would like for the *other* instruments to play to enhance the performance! In those days, we didn't use that title so prolifically as we do today, but Ritchie was actually producing his own records! He was a producer in every sense of the word. Some of the songs [on the first album] were done without arranging, with just him playing and us head-staff. He required a lot of takes because he was a severe critic of his own performance. Whenever he was unhappy with the performance, we would have to go back and do it over again. But it was *he* who was the critic, not Bob Keane or the other musicians."

Up to the time that he was recording demos for Del-Fi, Ritchie continued to use a small turquoise-green and white electric guitar called a "Harmony Stratotone," manufactured by Sears, but purchased from a pawn shop. He also had another electric guitar, probably of the Gibson variety, of which little is known. By the time Ritchie was in full swing with Del-Fi, he was performing on a Fender "Sunburst" Stratocaster for the most part. Hall recalled that Ritchie also played acoustical guitar at the sessions, although Keane could only remember Ritchie performing on electric guitar. "As far as Ritchie's proficiency as a guitarist," said Hall, "he wasn't a *technical* guitarist, but a *creative* guitarist. He was strictly creative and sometimes he would say certain things I wouldn't understand [musically].

"From the standpoint of a folk/Latin/Mexican style, he was very prolific. He loved to play in the key of D because he had the open A and D strings he could manipulate." Ritchie also liked to capo up third and fourth frets and Hall remembered an event at which Ritchie completely untuned his guitar: "He did one tune where his voice was too high and we wanted to do it in D flat and he couldn't play it. So, to go down to D flat, Ritchie just untuned the guitar and solved the problem that way."

Hall felt that like many other artists he worked with, Ritchie was handicapped by not knowing how to play in all keys. "That's why you find many of his tunes in the same key," said Hall, "because these are the keys he was most comfortable with on his instrument.

"Ritchie wanted to play while he sang. He was very strange on that. He could only get the natural feel of the performance when he could play on the guitar. He once said, 'I have to feel this thing. I gotta play the guitar.' If he didn't play, then he didn't want to sing." According to Hall, this was somewhat out of the ordinary since in a recording often the guitar lead was dubbed separately from the voice. It is almost certain that Ritchie always sang and played guitar at the same time.

Hall attested that most of the songs Ritchie recorded were Ritchie's: "They were his tunes. He was making them up. He had them written on a piece of paper. He [would] put the paper on the music stand, play his guitar and sing." In accomplishing the orchestration of the recording performances, Hall added, "Ritchie would come up to Bob's office and he would play and sing these songs while Bob turned on the tape. Once I would get the tape, then [Ritchie] would run *another* tape and play back what [he] heard and he would play things of what he wanted the other instruments to play. Sometimes, they were not technically feasible. If he heard something, he wanted it whether technically he could play it or not. He figured you should figure out some way to do it. Then we would argue and I'd say, 'The bass doesn't go any lower than E, Ritchie,' and he'd say, 'Well, I've gotta have that D,' and I'd say, 'Well, put your whole line up higher!' We would go through this bit and then I'd talk him into inverting the line someway and he'd say, 'Okay. I'll live with that. All right. Anything. You make me happy and I'll make you happy.'"

The musical personnel on Ritchie's songs consisted of electric guitarists Rene Hall, Bill Pitman, Carol Kaye, and Irvin Ashby, a former member of the Nat King Cole Trio; Red Collender and Buddy Clarke for upright bass; drummer Earl Palmer; and Ernie Freeman playing a barely discernible piano on "La Bamba."

One of the musical instruments that especially characterized Ritchie Valens' recordings on Del-Fi was the dan-electro guitar. This guitar differs from other electric guitars in that it is tuned in the same register as an electric bass or exactly one octave below the regular electric or acoustical guitar, with six instead of the four strings found on the bass electric. Although the dan-electro shares the same register as the bass electric, its resonance differs. The dan-electro lacks the resonance of the bass electric or upright bass and has more of a "twangy" sound, giving it a unique color. Hall, who played the dan-electro for the most part on Ritchie's recordings, said, "I would describe it as a cross between the electric guitar and the bass electric, although in actual pitch, it is the same as the regular bass electric."

Often, an additional bass electric or an upright bass was added to the dan-electro in Valens' music, as well as an additional electric guitar and Ritchie's lead guitar. The overall dominance of these guitar sounds with the permeating resonance of the dan-electro is one of the basic characteristics of the "Valens sound." Besides Hall, Bill Pitman and Carol Kaye also played dan-electro on Valens' recordings.

Ritchie's relationships with the sessions musicians and their perceptions of his relationship with Bob Keane were apparently very good. Hall's perception of Ritchie's personality and abilities was described as follows:

"He was very enthusiastic, a very likeable person. He wasn't temperamental and he was one of the artists I enjoyed working with because of that. I can always remember his smile and pleasant attitude. He was a happy artist as opposed to many I worked with back then who were forever arguing and fussing that the music wasn't right. With Ritchie, if it wasn't right, he'd say, 'I know. Let's do it again. I think we can do it better than that. Come on! Come on! You can do it! Come on, man!' It would make you happy and Ritchie was the type of guy you wanted to please 'cause you'd like to see the way he reacted when he was pleased. That was one of the things I loved about Ritchie: really happy, especially when he did something [musically] and liked the way he did it. Boy! Was he enthusiastic when they'd play back [the recordings]! He would dance all around the place!"

Palmer recalled: "Ritchie was kind of shy. He realized that he was a newly found talent and had no ego whatsoever. He had a lot of humility. He was always asking questions, about whether his performance was okay, because many of the people we recorded with had been his idols. So he was concerned whether the musicians were impressed."

Ross felt that Ritchie Valens and Bob Keane got along very well:

"Whatever Bob told Ritchie to do, he was happy with. When Bob would say that was a good take, Ritchie asked to hear it. He'd listen to it, then say, 'Yeh. It is good.' In the studio, they got along fine. I didn't notice any squabbling. Ritchie was humble, like all of them back then." But according to Ross, the sessions at Gold Star differed when Keane was round. He added, "Unfortunately, they were never relaxed, fun dates. Keane was paid by the hour, I think fifteen to twenty dollars an hour, and he was out there to make sure that everything was done right and have it all done. There were never any light moments. Keane was a worker. He didn't mess around with levity. Like Eddie Cochran, his were fun dates. He was here every week cutting demos for the American Music Corporation, under contract to Jerry Capehart. Jerry was relaxed and he was always telling corny jokes."

Apart from the regular recording sessions, apparently Ritchie and Rene Hall were working together on snatches of musical ideas, which, according to Hall, were put on a tape recorder that Ritchie had given him. He said, "Just before he left to go on that tour, we had done some overdubbing at Gold Star one evening and I saw Ritchie in the alley. That's when he gave me this tape recorder. He had communicated some [musical] ideas and we had put them on a little tape, because I was very busy at the time. After his unfortunate demise, I just discarded them because I never thought they'd be important to go through since he couldn't sing it."

Hall remembered one musical idea which had nothing to do with the fateful tape but was probably recorded in a demo which heretofore has been unreleased. He is assertive about the following story:

"The strangest thing that Ritchie did and I've never seen it on any of his albums is he composed the original background line to "Spanish Harlem"! Because I *remember* when we did it! He did that in one of his sessions. I don't think Bob Keane ever released a record of us doing it or maybe Ritchie didn't complete the melody for it. Ritchie didn't compose the *tune* [the melody of the song "Spanish Harlem"]. He composed that particular background line, which has been the main selling coin of the tune. I think it got out. Maybe Bob sold it, who knows?

"I remember that one little line because Ritchie taught it to *me* on the guitar. I would also remember it because in the key that he sung the line in—it was D—it was very difficult to get the brilliancy he was looking for. It was a duo line. If I played it on the inside strings, it didn't have the brilliancy because it started on an F sharp, and went down to D."

Hall explained that it was played an octave higher on the piano and played at a lower range on the inside strings of the guitar. He mentioned that Ritchie wanted it played on the guitar as on the piano. They worked out a compromise in which it would be played on the inner guitar strings in first inversion, so as to give more brilliancy to the line and to get the F sharp in the harmonic line. As Hall put it, "Ritchie told me, 'As long as I can

hear the F sharp, I don't care.' I played it that way and he was very happy with it."

Hall felt he maintained a very special relationship with Ritchie. He said, "I felt a tremendous loss when that happened [Ritchie's death]. Not from a financial standpoint because I didn't make that much from him, like I made from Sam Cooke, but I felt that he was eventually going to be something that was *different* from anything that I had worked with. The fact that he liked me and could communicate with me was there. I was one of the ten orchestrators that had the patience to sit down and give the artist *exactly* what he wanted, whether I liked him personally or not. This is what represented the difference to Ritchie. He said, 'I like you. You write what *I* want!' This is one reason I felt we would have gotten along famously had he come back."

*   *   *

After the initial audition, Doug Macchia was scheduled to continue work with Ritchie and Bob Keane, but this never came about. He said, "Bob and I got into a little hassle. Also, my father had become very ill and I had to drop out of the picture. Bob called me several times because I was supposed to manage Ritchie. He really didn't want to [manage Ritchie]. I didn't want to with the problems at home. Also, the legal age was twenty-one and I was twenty. I knew Ritchie was going to do well and I knew he would be great, but I couldn't handle it at the time.

"The reason Keane and I had a falling-out was that we were going to set up a circuit of concerts and I would provide Ritchie for them. At the time, Ritchie looked to me a little bit and Bob looked to me to guide Ritchie. This happened between the audition and the other sessions. Keane was also supposed to provide a bunch of big-name stars. We did our first one in San Fernando and it bombed, completely! It was at one of the movie theaters. I was a good friend of the theater manager and he wanted to try the show first. The manager had some trailers made up [Macchia believed that none of these trailers featured Ritchie]. Ritchie performed twice and he didn't get paid for it. That was the last time I saw Ritchie at the theater. Other than the phone calls to me, asking to manage Ritchie which came almost a month later, that was the end of my relationship with the whole thing."

5

THE STORIES BEHIND THE SONGS, I

"Well, come on, let's go, let's go . . ."

The exact dates of the Del-Fi recording sessions are not known, although there is a likelihood that the majority of them occurred during the summer of 1958. "Come On, Let's Go" first appeared as the "Pick of the Week" in *Billboard* magazine on Sept. 1, 1958. *Billboard* described the song this way:

"Ritchie, a new artist, has an effective approach on the rocker. Supported by good r 'n' r backing, he delivers the catchy tune which he cleffed himself in a saleable manner. It's a fine debut disc and the lad appears to have a winner with this first attempt."

The b/w side was "Framed," a Leiber/Stoller classic previously recorded by the Robins who eventually became the Coasters around 1956. Marna Publishing Company was the firm under which "Come On, Let's Go" was copyrighted and the only Valens song under that company. The other songs came under Kemo Music, in which Bob Keane was directly involved. The highest the DF4106 single reached was No. 42 on the *Billboard* charts in October, 1958. By November of that year, it was covered by Tommy Steele, the top British pop artist at the time. The song was later recorded by the McCoys in 1966 and most recently by the new wave group the Ramones in conjunction with the movie *Rock 'n' Roll High School* and by Los Lobos.

There is still a question whether "Come On, Let's Go" was recorded for final release in Keane's basement studio or at Gold Star. Bill Jones remembered it taking place at Keane's home. "I sat there for all fourteen takes of it," said Jones. "Keane had a really fine guitar player and when it came time for the guitar break, Ritchie dropped out and the other guitar player took it." Ritchie's brother, Bob Morales, confirms the story. "Ritchie didn't play the riff on 'Come On, Let's Go,'" said Morales. "Ritchie was a good player but he hadn't learned to pick the riff yet, so he played rhythm guitar.'"

The guitar break in the middle of the song belonged to Rene Hall who said it was his solo. Hall also stated that two saxophones, a tenor and a baritone, were on the recording, but the final mixing made them totally indiscernible. He remembered Tess Johnson and Jules Grant as the respective saxophonists. Red Collender thinks he played stand-up bass on the recording, but the drummer was definitely Earl Palmer.

As previously mentioned, "Come On, Let's Go" is one of the earliest songs more or less everyone agreed Ritchie wrote himself, though the words changed, even after it was commercially recorded, as in the version sung on the Pacoima Junior High School concert album. The origin of the phrase, according to Sandoval, came about when two Black students at a Pacoima Junior High assembly went up to Ritchie and said, "Come on, let's go!" from which he began the song. But the phrase is consistently used among Ritchie's family and its origin probably stems from Ritchie rather than anyone else.

An acquaintance of Bob Keane, Carter Saxon, played a special role in financing many of the Valens songs and especially "Come On, Let's Go." Saxon agreed to finance Keane in the making of the record after Keane informed him that a San Fernando music store owner would guarantee to sell one to two hundred of Ritchie's records. Keane took that number of records out to the store and began to get responses from all over the Hispanic community in the area. Then a radio station in Los Angeles, possibly KFWB, received calls wanting to hear more of "Come On, Let's Go." "I also guaranteed payment for the pressings of the song," said Saxon. He recalled that RCA was the company that pressed the record and that he extended credit for the bill of lading because, as he said, "They didn't trust Keane."

Doug Macchia believed that Cassel's Records in San Fernando was the store where the first promotion occurred. Although Macchia could not remember his name, a man who worked for the store went up and down the West Coast promoting Ritchie's record.

Chaubet had a special memory of when "Come On, Let's Go" was aired for the first time on radio. Apparently, there was a small house where he and Ritchie used to hang out. "I forgot the name of the street," said Chaubet, "but it was a little house and it had a cellar in it. We repainted the cellar with the money we got from Keane, put carpeting down in it—we even talked about a fish tank. Keane told Ritchie that the song was going to air Tuesday but didn't say when." Chaubet said that particular night, he and Ritchie were in the refurnished cellar waiting for the song to air: "About five to twelve, we heard it [Come On, Let's Go] and I didn't even know it was him! They put a lot of echo in the song. It was on KFWB radio, I'm pretty sure."

Donna Fox also remembered the first time she heard the song on the radio: "I remember [beforehand] Ritchie walking up to me in school and telling me that he had recorded his first record and that they had changed his name to Ritchie Valens. I laughed and really didn't believe him because I thought he was kidding me. One day, I was driving down the street in San Fernando with a carload of my girlfriends and all of a sudden, this song comes on the radio and there it was: Ritchie as big as life! I just about died! I couldn't believe it!" Donna Fox also remembered that Ritchie did a concert at San Fernando High shortly after the song was released.

The "Pacoima version," the only known version of "Come On, Let's Go" outside of the commercial Del-Fi recording, is one of two audible proofs that Ritchie continued to create songs from the same basic phrases, making them up simultaneously. No doubt Keane was puzzled as to *why* Ritchie never sang "Come On, Let's Go" [or any other song, as a matter of fact] the same way twice. It is probably safe to assume that Ritchie as well did not know why he changed a song from one performance to the next, other than for the satisfaction of doing it. Whether directly or indirectly, Ritchie's exposure to traditional Mexican music, especially the *sones* and *huapangos*, which are characterized by variations on basic melodic modal patterns, makes "Come On, Let's Go" in a sense "Mexican." The chart below compares the two known versions of the song:

	Del-Fi (DF 4106)	*Pacoima Version*
Harmonic rhythm:	same	same
Beginning vocal intonation (on 5th interval):	same	same
Rhythmic continuity:	constant	somewhat freeform

	Del-Fi (DF 4106)	*Pacoima Version*
Tempo:	same	same
Words:	very set, formulated	created simultaneously, almost nonsensical
Guitar riffs:	very few	consistent with those in later Valens demos

In addition, the continual use of pure I, IV, V [tonic, sub-dominant, dominant] chords throughout the song within each 8-bar phrase, in which the I chord gets four beats, the IV, two, and the V, two, can be considered another element that lends the "Mexican" flavor to what can be characterized as the Valens style. The guitar breaks carried by Hall in the commercial version are like punctuating sounds of blues between the stirring I, IV, V sequence. Palmer's strong basic drumming accentuates the rock 'n' roll aspect of the whole song, in a way that would be found later in "garage-band" pieces of the 60's.

"I had a girl, Donna was her name . . ."

While "Come On, Let's Go" was going fairly strong on the *Billboard* charts, Keane decided to release two other songs sometime around October, 1958. They were "Donna" b/w "La Bamba," Del-Fi 4110. Both first appeared in the *Billboard* "Spotlight" November 17, 1958. The song that was reputed to have been recorded on Keane's Ampex tape recorder in his basement went to the No. 2 position by January, 1959. By February of that year, "Donna" slid down within the top ten charts, but by the first week of March, it went back up to No. 2. Ironically, Ritchie's first album was also released the first week of that month [March 9, 1959], exactly one month and six days after his death.

It is this simple little song, written for a sixteen-year-old high school acquaintance, that is most associated with Ritchie Valens and yet, within the simple framework of "Donna" lies a wide range of controversy and dispute, ranging from for whom the song was originally intended to who actually wrote the song. Even the relationship Ritchie may have had with Donna Ludwig [Fox] is in question. One friend who knew them both well stated frankly, "I know that Donna was just using Ritchie. She was kind of embarrassed to be seen with him." Most of Ritchie's acquaintances seemed to agree that Donna and Ritchie were not very close. Another mutual friend, John Alcaraz, agreed: "I knew the guy that Donna was dating. Donna was one of those real good-looking girls in school, the type that everybody wanted to go out with and later on she met Ritchie. Ritchie always wanted to go out with her but I don't think he ever did. He liked her. That's why the song came out. I guess he did the best thing he could do—write a song for her."

Most of the Silhouettes felt that Ritchie and Donna were not that close. Préndez recalled, "I used to see Donna at the hamburger drive-in in San Fernando but I didn't know that Ritchie was involved with her until he started with the song." Aguilera added, "He was real serious about Donna but I don't know if Donna was serious about him." Aguilera and the other Silhouettes also knew about Donna's father's initial feelings about Ritchie [because of his ethnic background] and he said, "We knew something about that but we didn't want to get involved. That was his [Ritchie's] business."

Donna herself admitted that she and Ritchie never really dated. She said, "For some reason, my father didn't care too much for him and I wasn't allowed to date him. I had to sneak and meet him at parties and roller skating rinks. It got to be quite a hassle."

Despite the difficulties which may or may not have been racially motivated, Donna did admit that there was a close relationship between her and Ritchie. "It was all a very simple, teenage type of thing," she said. "We just had a nice little relationship. Of course, we necked and that was average but we were never deeply sexually involved."

She recalled the names of some of the places she, Ritchie and their friends used to hang out—Bob's Drive-In (Van Nuys) and Big Boy (she remembered Van Nuys; others remembered San Fernando, though that particular location is officially Mission Hills), and the Rainbow Roller Rink in Van Nuys (presently an ice skating rink). Donna's recollection of how the song came about is the following:

"In the interim, we had a little falling-out and Ritchie was seeing a girl who is now my stepsister, but my girlfriend at the time, Cathy Brown. I can't remember why we had the argument; however, one night Ritchie called me and sang me a song. A few years after Ritchie's death, I was led to believe that someone else had written Ritchie's recording of 'Donna,' but I can *swear* that I talked to him on the phone and he sang it with his guitar in the background. Let people say what they want, I know he wrote it for me."

Mrs. Reyes also attested that Ritchie was close to Donna. She stated that Ritchie was at her home the time the song was sung over the phone: "Ritchie told me, 'Look, *tía*, I made this song and it's going to be for Donna.' So he phoned her and started telling her about it. Then he actually sang the song for her over the phone." Mrs. Reyes also remembered that later on the road, Ritchie told her that he had a "bet" with members of the Crests, who had their first hit, "Sixteen Candles," as to whose song was going to make it to No. 1 first.

Donna Fox also had another story to tell about the song:

"The song was recorded but hadn't been distributed yet. Ritchie was introducing 'Donna' and they had a big dance and converted the Rainbow Roller Rink into a dance hall. I wanted to look extra nice so I bought a bright red outfit. Ritchie liked red on me with my blond hair. As soon as he got through playing, he came down and put his arm around me, introducing me to all the band members and said, 'This is my girl.' Then 'Donna' was released and the first time I heard it, I bawled like a baby. It was quite touching."

Too many people have laid claim to the origin of the song. Several have attributed that, at most, Ritchie had a minimal part in the writing of "Donna." Perhaps, the most surprising of these claims comes from a book by Richard Williams, *Out of His Head*, in which none other than Phil Spector has claimed to have had a hand in the production of "Donna." Spector attended Fairfax High School in Hollywood and was part of a group called the Teddy Bears which had a hit, "To Know Him Is to Love Him," a few months before "Come On, Let's Go" was released. It remained a hit after "Donna" was released. Therefore, the possibility of Spector and Valens meeting each other while performing the L.A. circuit is feasible. There is an uncanny resemblance in rhythm and orchestration between the two songs, but the possibility of Spector, who at the time, was barely organizing his own musical affairs, to have had even a small part in the making of "Donna" (other than Ritchie possibly listening to "To Know Him Is to Love Him") is highly improbable.

Bob Keane had this to say about "Donna": "He had only the very first line: 'I had a girl, Donna was her name,' and that's all he ever had, with a couple of four- or eight-bar riffs. I and my partner in the publishing business wrote the rest of the song. I didn't take credit for Ritchie's songs, except for maybe one or two." Keane mentioned he co-wrote many of the Valens songs under the pseudonym of "R. Kuhn," in actuality, his real name. Keane also said that it was his voice that dubbed in the harmonized part of not only "Donna" but other songs as well. He said, "I wanted to overdub Ritchie's voice at the beginning but I couldn't get him to do it. He said, 'I can't do it.' He wouldn't try." However, Hall said that Ritchie did sing his own harmonies on the dubbing and emphasized that Keane was not a singer or a guitarist. Keane went on to say that additional refinements were done to the basement recording: "I used professional microphones and crossed the circuits to get the echo and all I had there was Ritchie on his guitar. Then I took it into the studio and put on not Rene, but another guy playing rhythm guitar. Ritchie made the fills; there was a bass player [Clark] and the drummer [Palmer]."

The claim about who actually wrote "Donna" transcends Keane's possible role—there is some dispute among members of the Silhouettes.

Conrad Jones, the younger brother of Bill, wrote, "Ritchie did not write 'Donna.' I did and only for one person in the world—Richard Valenzuela—who was in love very much with a girl who really didn't love him." But his brother had a different story behind the song: "The original guy who wrote 'Donna' was Gilbert Royale who is currently in East L.A. He wrote a song called 'Emma' [after Emma Franco, the Silhouettes' singer] and the only thing Richard did was drop 'Emma' and put in 'Donna.' He took it word for word the way Gilbert wrote it. There was no change in it, just the name only. If anybody else was feeling blue and wanted to use the song, he would put his own girl's name in there. But originally, it was written by Chico [nickname of Gilbert Royale]."

Other Silhouettes disagreed and claimed that Royale was not really a musician but hung around them. Also, the song was originally called 'Mercy,' after Mercy Ortiz (married Harfield), Armando Ortiz' sister whom Conrad supposedly had a crush on. The song which eventually became "Donna," was apparently a joint effort. Aguilera said, "They [Conrad/Bill] had written a song, called 'Mercy.' Richard used that and kind of made it into 'Donna.' That is the truth and I remember that much, but in my opinion, they all came up with it *together*. They all said 'Let's make it into 'Donna' and they did." Ortiz agreed that Conrad wrote most of the song (as "Mercy") and Ritchie changed it, but Gallardo believed that Ritchie wrote the whole song. Préndez added, "It was at the Joneses' house; we went [there] one night and the song came to be. It was called 'Mercy,' because Conrad had a crush on her. But one night, Keane was at their house and the song changed to 'Donna.' Conrad gave Ritchie the words and Ritchie started using 'Donna' in Mercy's place. I might add that Takaki also had a crush on Mercy, so I would suppose that Ritchie, Conrad and Walter [Takaki] all made the song possible as far as the *words*. The *tune* of the song, I would have to say that was all Ritchie's."

Takaki also agreed with Préndez' story and added, "It was written one night when we all got together and Keane was with us. We had just played at a dance. Ritchie played it at the Joneses' place with the rhythm and everything and Keane said, 'Hey! That sounds good! Why don't we build up words around it?' So we all got together and it was just a simple song called 'Mercy.' That's where the words came from and that's where Ritchie got them. As for Ritchie singing the song on the phone to Donna, well, that part is true, but he never quite sang it the way it was in the [original] song."

In a way, "Donna" is somewhat atypical for one referred to as the "Little Richard of the Valley." Ritchie was more accustomed to singing rockers than ballads. The sentimentality found in "Donna" was not as common in other Valens compositions. In light of the question about whether the song was written by someone else or a joint effort of the Silhouettes, it must be pointed out that the words do seem more "prosaic" than the traditional Valens style. Yet, it must be remembered that the essence of the Valens sound was to change the words and sometimes the melody, while keeping the basic theme of the song.

There is also a possibility that "Donna" emanated from another source—it does bear a strong melodic resemblance to Lee Andrews and the Hearts' "Teardrops," which became a hit around November, 1957. In listening to Ritchie's ballads, "Donna," "We Belong Together," "Now You're Gone," etc., one recognizes that they all stem from rhythm and blues roots. There is a curious fanzine story that relates to it all. A girl had won a KFWB contest with an evening with Ritchie Valens as the prize. The story goes on to mention that Ritchie sang a song with this girl called "Edna," a rather obscure rhythm and blues ballad by the Medallions. This is not as unusual as it may appear, considering that the girl and her friends came from a middle-class Anglo neighborhood. At the time, an L.A. disc jockey named Huggy Boy had been spinning such r 'n' b rarities as "Edna," many of which in later years came to be known as "doo-wop." So by 1958, partially due to Huggy Boy's show, the L.A. area was one of the few in the country that had a conscious awareness on the part of its rock 'n' roll fans of earlier rhythm 'n' blues sounds. Irrespective of ethnicity or location within the L.A. area, many teenagers were knowledgeable of black r 'n' b performers, whether or not their songs reached the national top charts. Their ballad sounds were being emulated by young performers of all races. "Donna" was no exception. Its roots were pure r 'n' b and whether it was a variation of "Teardrops" or an earlier ballad created by members of a local San Fernando Valley band, it bears a special Valens quality that can hardly be called imitative—the almost pure use of I, IV, V chords, against an occasional blues guitar riff, especially on the pickup following the phrase, "after all the time my love for you" (Hall mentioned that Ritchie thought this particular melodic line was more "bluesy" than the typical Valens sound!). "Donna" contains a vocal solo rich enough to retain a "doo-wop" sound, without the group, so to speak. Sandoval recalled that when Ritchie performed "Donna" in person, he would sometimes hold out certain words, retaining the triplet rhythmic beat (common in many late '50's ballads), but losing the basic 4/4 meter of the piece. For example, in the phrase, "I don't know what I'd do," the word *know* would get four counts of triplets (i.e., 3 3 3 3), instead of three counts as in the recording (i.e., 3 3 3). Other words, particularly at the ends of phrases, sometimes received the same treatment.

Around the same time "Donna" was created, Ritchie and Bob Keane took a trip to San Francisco, continuing to promote "Come On, Let's Go." On their way back, they stopped at a home rented by Carter Saxon in Carpinteria. Saxon said, "My daughter, then about thirteen years old, and some of her friends were up there. Ritchie had his guitar without the electrical hookup but he strummed it and also sang. The kids sat there and listened while he played "La Bamba" and three or four other songs. Then he played "Donna" and my daughter Helen said, 'If that was a record, I'd buy it!' and I said, 'Bob, why don't you cut that?' He said, 'No, it's too early to have Ritchie sing a love song. Gotta have another driver first. I'm going to cut "La Bamba." I replied, 'Swell! "La Bamba's" great, but why don't you put "Donna" on the flip side?' And so, Keane did that and they both took off. Locally, they were numbers 1 and 2 on the charts for weeks."

"Donna" had its influence within the popular music world. It was covered in England by Marty Wilde, one of the top artists in 1959, and ironically, Del-Fi covered its own song in 1962-63, sung by Johnny Crawford, the young star of the TV series "Rifleman." The song seemed to have influenced other songs, especially its namesakes, such as Dion's 1963 hit, "Donna, the Primadonna," and even the notorious song about Donna (the Virgin) from the musical "Hair." The original song was again covered in the mid-70's by Donny Osmond and Freddy Fender. As Lester Bangs, the late *Rolling Stone* writer, said: "'Donna' is one of the classic teen love ballads, one of the few which reaches through layers of maudlin sentiment to give you the true and unmistakable sensation of what it may have been like to be a teenager in that strange decade."

"Yo no soy marinero . . . soy capitán . . ."

The song "La Bamba" is one of the few songs that is the fiber of Mexican folklore. Traditionally a wedding dance from the region of Veracruz, it is often performed to this day in all its original regalia even at weddings north of the border. The origin of the name "bamba" is African, meaning "wood" (language is not known, though there is a people and even several towns throughout Africa called "Bamba"). The "wood" referred to what the dancers originally performed upon, emphasizing footwork that showed a heavy Spanish influence. The highlight of the dance would be one solo couple tying a ribbon, just using their feet, to symbolize marriage/unity. The song itself is an old *huapango* at least sixty years old or older. A *huapango* is a Mexican song consisting of nonsense verses, which usually have undertoned meanings, many times often private in context. Such is the case of "La Bamba."

When the traditional dance is not performed at a wedding, often the band will play "La Bamba" in a more popular vein, changing the original 16/8 tempo to 4/4 time. The popular rendition has been performed in America since World War II, yet in spite of all the Latin popular songs which became renowned in the 30's and 40's, "La Bamba" was apparently not successfully recorded until 1958, with Ritchie Valens' version.

Ritchie's relationship to "La Bamba" goes back to at least Pacoima Junior High, where both students and teachers remembered his playing it. Ritchie in return learned it from Richard "Dickie" Cota, his cousin, who supposedly played many of the familiar riffs and chords in similar fashion.

Sandoval recalled, "When Ritchie used to play 'La Bamba,' he would play in loose, shifting meters. It wasn't a straight 4/4 or 3/4 time and I had a hard time playing it that way because I learned it from him like that." The rhythm on the guitar that Sandoval described went something like the following example:

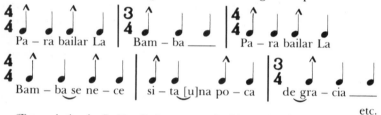

(Transcription by B. Mendheim, as sung by Manny Sandoval)

"He used to play it as fast as he could," said Sandoval. He used to go really fast. The rock version came much later."

Mrs. Reyes agreed with Sandoval's recollections but added that Ritchie's version was plainer with different words. Ritchie sang "La Bamba" one way, "and that was the rock and roll way," she said.

Both Rene Hall and Stan Ross remembered "La Bamba" done at Gold Star Studios. Hall remembered going into the studio to do the commercial recording shortly after the home tape session of "Donna." Said Ross, "Probably no more than four takes were done on 'La Bamba.' It was done live." Hall played dan-electro which comes in as a leading melodic line with Ritchie's lead guitar; other musicians at the session were Irving Ashby, rhythm guitar; Buddy Clarke, upright bass (Red Collender also claimed he played upright bass on "La Bamba"); Carol Kaye, electric guitar; Earl Palmer, drums, wood block. Hall recalled that there was also a piano at the session, played by Ernie Freeman, who remembered being there playing a first inversion riff on the upper registers of the instrument. This riff is barely discernible on the actual recording, even when an equalizer is employed to filter out the treble parts of the song. Freeman also remembered some overdubbing done on the song, although both Hall and Ross maintain that the session was done live. Keane also agreed on the overdubbing process:

"We used three or four tracks then. We laid down the rhythm with Ritchie on guitar because he was the driving force in the rhythm section. Then we put his voice on the second track. He used a hand-held mike (contrary to what was said about Ritchie playing guitar while singing). On the third track, Rene played a dan-electro bass, dubbed it right on top of the upright bass pattern to give it a more percussive sound."

According to Hall (and also Ritchie's brother Morales who was at the session), Ritchie played both the beginning guitar riff and solo guitar break on "La Bamba." An important characteristic of the sound is due to the thickness of the heavy gauge strings Ritchie probably used on his guitar. The song was done in the key of F.

Keane maintained that Ritchie did not initially want to record "La Bamba" because, as Keane said, "Ritchie felt it would demean his culture. It was a national folk song and he was afraid it would be exploiting his ethnic music. He was funny that way." But Keane also mentioned that Ritchie may have been following the feelings of his mother about commercially recording "La Bamba." The "cultural awareness" Ritchie may have personally had about the song is highly debatable in the light of the times. In the '50's those of Mexican heritage did not always identify themselves as such and the term "Chicano" was considered somewhat derogatory. Also, although locally known, it was not generally known that Ritchie was of Mexican extraction until after his death. Yet, being a musician, Ritchie probably had more of a cultural sensitivity than normal for most teens of his background, even those belonging to restrictive clubs or gangs.

Another problem was Ritchie's Spanish. He may have been reluctant to record the song because of his Spanish. "Ritchie had an accent when he sang 'La Bamba,'" said Morales. "The words were mispronounced. Keane was behind him whispering the words to him! But I liked the way Ritchie played it."

"La Bamba" first appeared on the *Billboard* charts in late December, 1958. It was the highest around the weeks ending

January 19 and 26, and February 2, 1959. It began to fluctuate the following month and by April of that year, it just about disappeared while "Donna" stayed on. In later years, "La Bamba" was revitalized by people in the folk scene such as the Kingston Trio, Joan Báez, and Harry Belafonte. Trini López made it a hit again in 1966, with a lighter rock-pop sound to it than originally recorded. Other pop and rock performers, including the post-Holly Crickets, made versions of the song and it was combined throughout dance halls with a 1962 hit (with a strikingly similar melody) made famous by the Isley Brothers called "Twist and Shout." There is even a disco version of "La Bamba" and recently an L.A. group called the Plugz recorded a punk rock version based on Valens' original riffs. Although the new wave group the Ramones did not record "La Bamba," the song is considered, along with "Come On, Let's Go," a forerunner of their hit, "Blitzkrieg Bop."

"La Bamba" had been accepted as a popular song long before Ritchie recorded it and it is a puzzle why it was never recorded in this country earlier. Had not Valens recorded it, someone inevitably would have, but the orchestration would probably not have been as successful in converting a traditional musical selection into a popular vein. The use of a rock and roll, rather than a Latin, percussion, with the predominance of compact and heavily layered guitar sounds (which in fact replace the common r 'n'r sax backgrounds), nonetheless retaining the essence of the Latin element, made this version by far one of the strongest sounds the late fifties ever put forth.

Professionally taken shots distributed by Del-Fi records. Originally, the family had the shot at upper left taken by a private studio. Photos: Ernestine Reyes collection.

Ritchie performing on a TV show, probably "The Music Shop," January 11, 1959. Photo: Ernestine Reyes collection.

Ritchie with manager Bob Keene (Keane) reading about himself in *Music Vendor* (which no longer exists). Probably taken in late 1958. Photo: Ernestine Reyes collection.

Lobby card for the film *Go Johnny Go!* This was Alan Freed's last movie, released in the summer of 1959. Ritchie is on the left, second up from bottom. Original is in color, ©1985, courtesy of Hal Roach Studios, Inc. Black and white photo by S. Guitarez.

Promotional shot for the film *Go Johnny Go!* (Jan. [?] 1959). Ritchie wore a different tweed sport coat in the final version of the film. Photograph courtesy of Hal Roach Studios, Inc.

Ritchie performing on stage, Winter Dance Party tour, Eagles Ball-room, Kenosha, Wisconsin, January 24, 1959. Photo: Robert Sterel-cyzk.

Professionally taken photo of Ritchie distributed by Del-Fi records. Autograph in upper left corner was written by Ritchie's mother for the Reyes family. Photo: Ernestine Reyes collection.

An intense moment on stage at the Eagles Ballroom performance (Kenosha, WI, Jan. 24, 1959). Waylon Jennings on guitar (far right). Photo: Robert Sterelcyzk.

Ritchie with local DJs Jim Lounsbury (left) and Ed Oxar (right), and Lounsbury's wife. Winter Dance Party tour, Eagles Ballroom, Kenosha, WI, Jan. 24, 1959. Photo: Robert Sterelcyzk.

Signing autographs at the end of the show (clockwise, from left): Ritchie, Dion, Big Bopper, Jim Lounsbury, and Frankie Sardo. Eagles Ballroom, Kenosha, WI, Jan. 24, 1959. Photo: Robert Sterelcyzk.

Ritchie on drums with Tommy Allsup (second from right) and Waylon Jennings (far right) on guitars. Riverside Ballroom, Green Bay, WI, Feb. 1, 1959. Originally in color, this is one of the last known shots of Ritchie on the Winter Dance Party tour. Photo: Larry Matti.

Autographs of Buddy Holly, Ritchie Valens, the Big Bopper, and Frankie Sardo, given to Larry Matti on Feb. 1, 1959, Riverside Ballroom, Green Bay, WI. Photo: Larry Matti collection.

6

THE STORIES BEHIND THE SONGS, II

"Well, I had a girl . . ."—The "girl" songs

Aside from "Donna," Ritchie also recorded four other songs dealing with the topic of girls: "That's My Little Suzie," "Hi-Tone," "Little Girl," and "Boney-Maronie." Of the four, Ritchie often sang "That's My Little Suzie" and "Boney-Maronie" prior to his contract with Del-Fi.

"That's My Little Suzie," released as a single, was the first posthumous release, in March, 1959. *Billboard* called it "a rocker in the rockabilly tradition that really moves," in the March 23, 1959 issue; by May of that year, it had only reached No. 55. It was also released in England (as London HL8886) around the same time with a different b/w side, "Bluebirds Over the Mountain," from the American (DF 4114) release, "In a Turkish Town." It was recorded at Gold Star as part of the first album and later appeared in Valens EPs in both America and England.

Sometime around 1970, an earlier demo of this song, misnomered "Rock Little Donna," appeared on an album entitled *The Original Ritchie Valens*, Guest Star 1469. This particular version was identified by Macchia as one of the demos sung at the audition. Were it not for this surviving demo, the background of "That's My Little Suzie" would have remained more of an enigma. Although the polished Del-Fi version was said to be cowritten by Kuhn (a.k.a. Keane), the demo is, in the purest sense, strictly Ritchie Valens, with verses seemingly composed "on the spot."

Who the song was for remains a mystery. A former schoolmate from Pacoima suggested that it may have been for a "Suzie Rosas" who attended Pacoima Junior High and who was close to Ritchie at the time. However, neither Sandoval nor anyone else in the Silhouettes could recall a "Suzie Rosas." In addition, Mrs. Reyes, who could not remember who the song was written for, did assert that it was not for a "Suzie Rosas." Donna Fox doubted that the song was for her under a pseudonym, although she did tell an interesting story behind one of the lines of the demo:

> "She jus' shakes me all over my head,
> When she gets me doin' the hen . . ."
> ("Rock Little Donna")

She said, "Ritchie was an excellent dancer—he did swing dance and slow dance really good, but he used to do some silly little thing: put his hands under his armpits, like 'flapping his wings,' like a chicken. He did that as a joke and I used to tell him he looked silly."

According to a promo sheet Del-Fi published for the first album, *Ritchie Valens*, the idea of the polished version came from a line of Little Richard's song, a song which is never mentioned. Keane said, "[The beginning riff] on 'Little Suzie' has the same feel as the Bo Diddley beat." This riff, however, is more akin to the beginning riff or motive found in an earlier song by the Everly Brothers, "Claudette," released in April, 1958. As well, the name "Suzie" is spelled the same way as the Everlys' "Wake Up, Little Suzie" (released a few months later from "Claudette"). These songs may suggest the origin of "That's My Little Suzie."

In comparing the two versions, "That's My Little Suzie" and "Rock Little Donna" are very dissimilar, except in one area: The *form* of the song is virtually the same, even though "Little Donna" is longer in content. Other facets of the two versions are compared in the following chart:

"That's My Little Suzie"	*"Rock Little Donna"*
Guitar riff/motive connecting the whole song, with a few Chuck Berry riffs mostly in the break.	No specific guitar riff/motive connecting song together. Plenty of Chuck Berry riffs.
FORM: A A^1 B A^2 (break) B A^2	FORM: A A^1 B A^2 (break) B A^2
Strong use of minor 3rd interval	Strong use of major chords, except for occasional "flat 7th."
WORDS: plaintive/repetitive	WORDS: very narrative/topical

Outside of the two guitars (Valens and Hall—it is suspected Ritchie played lead) and drums (Palmer), the instrumentation for the commercial version of "That's My Little Suzie" is unknown. Possibly Buddy Clarke or Bill Pitman played stand-up bass, which would make a sufficient ensemble for the recording.

Another "girl" song which appeared as the third cut on the "B" side of the first album was called "Hi-Tone" and contained the highly unlikely musical arrangement of a neo-ragtime piano, possibly played by Ernie Freeman, two guitars (Valens and Kaye), a stand-up bass (Clarke or Pitman), and the soft drumming of Earl Palmer. According to the promotional sheet, "Hi-Tone" was written by a friend of Keane, Al Hazan, especially for Valens to sing. Supposedly, Ritchie liked it well enough to want it on his album, because, in his own words, "It kind of reminds me of junior high school."

The feel of the song is a light pop rock style, somewhat reminiscent of the early Ricky Nelson songs. Keane said, "It wasn't really Ritchie's song and he never should have done it. I didn't know any better in those days. It was [too] pop. They didn't call it then but it was almost a 'bubblegum' song."

However, Chaubet confided that Ritchie was in fact seeking variety in songs: "Ritchie wanted someone to write for him because he had so much in the way of his own songs." Also, some of Ritchie's own ideas may have been brought to Keane, who completed them by passing them onto selected songwriters. Donna Fox felt that "Hi-Tone" may have also been for her. She said, "I'm very nearsighted and in school I was vain, never wore glasses. People would wave at me and I wouldn't see them or I would just walk by and people would think I was conceited. Ritchie would laugh about it. He said once, 'Everybody thinks you got your nose stuck in the air,' and I would reply, 'No, I don't. You know that!'"

"Hi-Tone" was, with its bouncy piano backup, probably the most "pop" song that Ritchie recorded and yet he was able to pull it off quite convincingly as if it had all the soul of a standard rhythm 'n' blues number. It remains one of the perfect examples of the Valens eclecticism.

"Little Girl," which appeared as the first cut on the "B" side of the second album, *Ritchie*, is also of the light pop rock vein. It has a musical arrangement similar to "Hi-Tone," but with a more pronounced use of guitars, especially in the riffs where a lead electric and dan-electro play in unison. There is also an echo-reverb, giving the song stronger depth.

The instrumentation of the song is vocal and guitar, with Valens playing either lead riff or rhythm; dan-electro played by Kaye; rhythm guitar, Valens or Hall; piano, possibly Freeman; stand-up bass, possibly Collender; and drums, Palmer. "Little Girl" is said to have been written by both Valens and "Kuhn" and the notes on the second album state that the song "was written around Ritchie's various phrases of speech." "Little Girl" appeared as a single (DF 4117) and as the follow-up release to "That's My Little Suzie." The song barely made a dent in the *Billboard* charts as No. 92 in July, 1959. It disappeared shortly thereafter.

This was rather unfortunate because musically "Little Girl" was a good arrangement, especially with Ritchie's voice punctuated by guitar riffs played in unison. The influence of Elvis Presley is quite apparent, yet there is a retention of the Valens softness to the song. Outside of "Hurry Up," this is the only known recorded Valens song in which he modulates a whole step upward, i.e., from the key of A (on the turntable) to the key of B. Ritchie has some problems with the lower notes of the song but this weakness is overcome by a high timbre that is crystalline and pure.

The words of the song are strangely "Dylanesque"—they tell of a girl who hurt him so, but nevertheless he will be true even though eventually he will have to leave her. The idea is unusual for a song of the fifties, almost as if it contained a prophetic undertone.

Probably the most underrated of these "girl" songs was Ritchie's version of the Larry Williams 1957 classic "Boney-Maronie." There is some question as to why the song was never released as a single nor placed on any of the later "Greatest Hits" albums, since it is known that this song was one of Ritchie's favorites which he sang extensively before signing with Del-Fi. Even when "Come On, Let's Go" was released, it is known that Ritchie sang this song alongside his first hit at local record hops.

Rene Hall admitted that he wanted to arrange "Boney-Maronie" with Ritchie because he was also the arranger for the Williams version. This song is an unusual example since the "cover" version equates, if not supercedes, the original version. The tempo on Larry Williams' version is much faster and, at certain points, seems rushed; the tempo of Valens' version is more deliberate, more planned. The riff that characterizes the song, played by saxes on the Williams recording, is echoed on the dan-electro in the Valens interpretation. Sixth chords dominate Larry Williams' recording, whereas major thirds and open fifths backed by a few minor thirds in the melody are more prominent in Valens' rendition. Carol Kaye played dan-electro on the piece, backed by two electric guitars, the lead was possibly played by Valens and the rhythm played by either Pitman or Hall; a stand-up bass, possibly played by Clarke; and drums, Palmer.

Ernestine Reyes had special memories of Ritchie performing "Boney-Maronie." There was one humorous story surrounding that particular song:

"We were taking Ritchie to El Monte Legion Stadium (exact month was not recalled but it was at the time Ritchie had just signed with Del-Fi). We were on our way there and he was a nervous wreck. I had never seen that kid so nervous! Lelo felt maybe a little drink would calm his nerves, so we stopped and got Ritchie a fifth [of whiskey]. He was sipping it all the way up there. When he got on stage, oh, my God! He was a' tore up! He was able to maintain as far as singing was concerned, but this time was too much! He threw out everything he had singing "Boney-Maronie." He sang that song from the bottom of his toes! The people were just going crazy over it. I had never seen the Legion Stadium go that crazy.

"We have heard Ritchie sing in many places and wherever he appeared, he would always watch for me, to tell him if we were not hearing him loud enough. This time, I was there in the middle of the audience, motioning him to settle down a little. He was so loud, we thought he was going to hurt his voice or something. The minute we came out of there and took him into the car, Lelo scolded him so bad, saying, 'I don't ever want to hear you singing like that again!' Ritchie answered with a hoarse, 'okay, tío.' He could hardly talk!"

"I hope Ersel Hickey doesn't mind . . ."—The "copy" songs

In addition to songs written or cowritten, Ritchie also record-ed versions of recent hits. Ironically, none of these "copy" songs was Little Richard's and whether Keane did not want Ritchie to record Little Richard or not is not as important as Ritchie's writing a song *in the style* of the pioneer rocker. "Ooh, My Head" should therefore be considered a "copy" song as much as the previously recorded hits "Bluebirds Over the Mountain," "We Belong Together," "Paddiwack Song," (all hits in 1958), and "Framed" (a rhythm 'n' blues standard from 1952).

"Bluebirds Over the Mountain" was recorded in February, 1958, by Ersel Hickey. Ritchie recorded it for inclusion in the first album; however, the song was released as a single in 1959 on the English London records (HL 8886), with the b/w side being "That's My Little Suzie." Although the Valens rendition was rather unknown in the U.S., it did become a fairly successful hit in England.

The promotional pamphlet described "Bluebirds" as "always one of Ritchie's favorite tunes" and it noted that Ritchie supposedly said, "I hope Ersel Hickey doesn't mind" when he recorded it. Yet, in comparing the two versions, they are like night and day. Hickey's is strictly rockabilly, with rhythmic phrases very stanzaic and nondeviating and a voice slightly reminiscent of Buddy Holly. The overall musical treatment of the Valens rendition is more variable, with a unique beginning of a vibrant tambourine played by Palmer, who also played drums (the tambourine was mixed in later), which sets the slow chalypso beat of the piece. (Chalypso was a variant rock 'n' roll rhythm often used in the late 50's and early 60's which combined elements of the Latin "cha-cha-cha" with then popular Caribbean calypso.) The riff on the dan-electro, played by Carol Kaye, enters alongside the tambourine and connects the whole piece together. The rhythmic phrases of both instrumentation and vocal are very expressive and syncopated. A stand-up bass played by Collender backs it all.

"Bluebirds Over the Mountain" became a standard "best" for Ritchie Valens, although it is not known whether he ever sang it publicly; it has been included in all subsequent LP re-releases and all the Del-Fi and British (London) EPs.

The song "We Belong Together," written and recorded by Robert and Johnny in February, 1958, was supposedly (and likely) Ritchie's favorite tune in the first album. The melody line of Robert and Johnny's hit may have been based on an older standard, "Blue Moon." Valens' rendition was released as the b/w side of "Little Girl." This song was the inspiration for the title of a tribute story to Ritchie in the May, 1959, issue of *Photoplay*. Ritchie's version went virtually nowhere but, strangely, "We Belong Together" influenced two other songs: "You're the One," by Chris Montez (1960) and "It's Time to Go" by the Carlos Brothers (1960).

The reason why Ritchie considered this song his favorite is best explained by Donna Fox: "That was *our* song—in the very beginning. That was one of the first songs that I heard him sing at the party where I first met him. At school, during lunch period, we had half an hour to dance and they would always play that record (Robert and Johnny's version) and Ritchie would always come over and say, 'They're playing our song.' We would dance and he would sing that and close his eyes. On slow songs, he'd close his eyes a lot."

Again, the Valens rendition is quite unlike the original. Robert and Johnny's "We Belong Together" has a full echo-reverb and an orchestration which uses saxes against the lower registered vocals of the duo. The overall sound of the Valens version tends to lean toward the upper registers and the timbre of Ritchie's voice is decidedly very clear and high. Again, the danelectro, either played by Hall or Pitman, takes the sax lines, with a rhythm guitar backing by Valens, stand-up bass by Collender and drums by Palmer. In addition, there is another unique guitar sound—an acoustical rhythm guitar played by Carol Kaye, which she called "an old Epiphone de Armand Emperor guitar which gave Phil Spector his 'echo-space' sound."

Next to "La Bamba," "Paddiwack Song," a variation of the "Children's Marching Song," was the other song Ritchie was most reluctant to record. Keane remembered how it came about. He and his family, along with Ritchie, were returning from an engagement in San Francisco. Ritchie was in the back of the car picking out the melody of "The Children's Marching Song," and Keane said, "I've gotta record that, Ritchie," but Ritchie replied, "Aw, no. That's something my mother sang to me when I was little. I don't want to do that!" "I had a hell of a time getting him to record it," said Keane.

The song was not released immediately. About the same time (late October or early November, 1958), a movie came out called "The Inn of the Sixth Happiness" featuring "The Children's Marching Song," which became a mild hit. Despite this success, the Del-Fi rendition was not released as a single until 1960, as the b/w side of "Cry, Cry, Cry" (DF 4133). By then, "Paddiwack Song" had already been placed on Ritchie's second album.

"Paddiwack Song" is no children's song but a rocker in its own right, a bluesy effect with guitar licks played in the break by Valens himself. Outside of Palmer's fantastic sixteenth note drumming, little else is known as to who played what on this session. The other instrumentation consists of dan-electro, rhythm guitar and stand-up bass.

A prominent feature in the song is a slight drop in the voice at the end of each completed phrase, a style also considered typically "Valens." One curious feature is hearing Ritchie laugh after the seventh verse while singing, "knick, knack, paddiwack." The expressiveness that Ritchie put in this song may be due to the possibility that he was referring to *himself* as the "old man" of the song. The concept is not far-fetched, considering what Mrs. Reyes said: "We used to call him 'the old man,' because Ritchie looked and seemed older than he really was."

"Framed" was originally recorded by the Robins back in 1952, some of whose members went on to become the Coasters (the song appeared on the first Coasters album). According to Silhouette Frankie Gallardo, Ritchie used to sing this song solo at parties and at Silhouettes' functions. With Valens (and possibly Hall) doing lead guitar riffs, Kaye on rhythm guitar, Collender on stand-up bass, and Palmer on drums, this song became the b/w side of "Come On, Let's Go."

"Framed" is a Leiber and Stoller classic that tells of the experience, originally identified within the Black community that catered rhythm 'n' blues, of the singer of the song being framed for a crime he did not commit. Upon initially hearing the Valens rendition, one may think that Ritchie was imitating a Black accent. Being raised in Pacoima, this was basically the way Ritchie spoke, especially in comparing his speech level heard on the Pacoima Junior High School album. Ritchie treats his version of "Framed" as an incident that could have happened to any Chicano youth in Los Angeles or in any other place in California at the time. The song had a special relevance to the Black and Brown communities of the northern end of the San Fernando Valley. In addition, a bit of the Valens element is lent to the Leiber/Stoller song—the words are slightly changed, more simplified. In the Robins/Coasters version, the words go:

>"'Where were you in 1929?'
>'I was here, judge.'
>He said, 'That man's lying!'"
>(© 1952 Leiber/Stoller)

In the Valens version, they go:

>"'Where were you in July, 1953?'
>'I was jus' a' home, justa pleadin'!'"
>(Valens version, 1958)

The innovative expressiveness used in Ritchie's interpretation of "Framed" cannot be overlooked. Even though Ritchie himself may not have experienced the story of the song, the way he sings it is quite real.

*   *   *

Although Ritchie never recorded, as far as is known, any of the Little Richard songs he was noted for singing, he did record one in the style of Little Richard's "Ooh, My Soul" (May, 1958). It was "Ooh, My Head."

According to the promo sheet, the idea for the song came out of a six-hour recording date toward the end of November, 1958. During a break, Ritchie was sitting by himself, singing and playing what would later become "Ooh, My Head." When the musicians filed back, Keane motioned Ritchie to continue to play while the musicians joined him. Keane then cued the engineer to tape the session which went on for almost twelve minutes. Several weeks later, the tape was edited and the song put on the first album. Also, according to the promo sheet, Ritchie often used the expression "Ooh, my head hurts."

At some later time, Ritchie sang this song for Alan Freed, who decided to put it in his forthcoming movie *Go Johnny, Go.* (The description of the movie sequence is in Chapter 8.) "Ooh, My Head" was never released as a single in America, but in 1962 it was the b/w side of an English release of "La Bamba" (London/Decca HL9494). In 1975, British rock group Led Zeppelin picked up this song and included it in one of their albums. L.A. writer Jim Dawson best describes what happened:

"Nothing better underscores Valens' obscurity than the plundering of one of his songs, 'Ooh, My Head' by Led Zeppelin. The band retitled the song 'Boogie With Stu' and included it in its

Physical Graffiti album, listing themselves as composers. Luckily, Kemo Music, which owns the song, discovered Zeppelin's 'oversight' a year later and brought suit. On July 28, 1978, Kemo settled out of court with Zeppelin and Swan Song Records for a reported $130,000 plus future royalties with the stipulation that the settlement's incriminating terms be kept confidential. Though not a party in the suit, Valens' mother received half the money."

Mrs. Valenzuela's former attorney, Joseph Porter III, confirmed that "Ooh, My Head" was settled. However, it is not known whether Led Zeppelin included the name "Mrs. Valens" as the "composer" of "Boogie With Stu" before or after the settlement, though there is indication that it may have been done beforehand as a "joke" on the part of the rock group.

"Ooh, My Head" is probably one of Valens' best rockers. The blues progression is almost note for note imitative of Little Richard's "Ooh, My Soul," with some crucial differences. The guitar riffs in the break, played by Valens, are similar to the ones played in the beginning of "Come On, Let's Go" (originally played by Hall), and they lean more toward a Chuck Berry technique. The drums were played by Palmer and there were two guitars, one of which was played in a "boogie-woogie" rhythm, perhaps by Valens, and there was the use of a stand-up bass, but otherwise, no one really knows who played what on this selection. The song ends perfectly with a one-note syncopation on E while Valens states the expression, "Way-up!" (an expression later borrowed by Chris Montez in his hit "Let's Dance") and finally ends with, "My head's tired!"

"There across the sea . . ."—"In a Turkish Town" and "Dooby Dooby Wah"

Two remaining songs included on Ritchie's first album are special within themselves—"In a Turkish Town" and "Dooby Dooby Wah."

Probably one of the most unique songs to emerge from the late 50's is "In a Turkish Town." It is unique because of its song idea, its asymmetrical rhythm and shifting of meters, and its melody line. Yet, the story surrounding this song is as mysterious as its title may suggest. Although Bill Jones claimed that the song was originally recorded in Keane's basement set-up at the audition with overdubbings later put in, the chances are more likely that the whole song was recorded at Gold Star studios, with finger cymbals and bongo drums (to imitate the sound of the Middle Eastern drum, the *darabukka*), which may have been later dubbed in by Palmer. The rest of the instrumentation is very sparse with just a lead guitar (Valens), rhythm guitar (Hall), and a stand-up bass (possibly Collender). This song is another example in which it is known for sure that Ritchie played lead because as Hall attested, "On the solo break, that's him because I can tell his tremolo from mine. He used it much slower than I do." Bob Keane claimed that the harmony line in "Turkish Town" was his vocal, as in the other harmonies of Valens' songs, yet the voice pattern seems more like Ritchie's and probably was dubbed in rather than sung along with the leading melodic line.

There is considerable controversy as to who wrote the song. Both the Jones Brothers lay claim that Conrad wrote most of the song for Ritchie and Chaubet also made this claim, stating that Ritchie wanted to join a club at high school called "The Turks." It is not really known if there was a San Fernando High School group called the "Turks," but the graduating class of 1959, who donated a scoreboard to the school, called themselves "The Saracens." To help pay for that scoreboard, they sponsored Ritchie to play at a paid rally. There is also another story, according to the promo sheet, that "In a Turkish Town" was based upon a dream Ritchie had two years earlier about being on a flying carpet and that the first thing that came to Ritchie's mind was the exotic setting of Turkey. Mrs. Reyes distinctly recalled the time Ritchie sang the song to her: "He wanted me to hear it, to see how it sounded. I asked him that day, 'Where in the heck did you get that?' He told me he didn't know. He just made up the song."

Other Silhouettes claimed that "In a Turkish Town" was actually the joint efforts of both Conrad Jones and Ritchie. There is still another curious possibility about the song's origin: The beginning melodic line is not unlike the beginning of the melody for (of all things!) an Indonesian folk song, a children's song about an umbrella dance called "Tari Payung" or "Babendi Bendi." This idea would be considered farfetched and totally coincidental if not for the fact that there *was* an Indonesian foreign exchange student at San Fernando High around the time that Ritchie (and Conrad) were attending the school. Therefore, that possibility of this origin should not be ruled out.

"In a Turkish Town" was the b/w side of the single "That's My
Little Suzie." Although "Turkish Town" was never released separately in England, sometime in the early 60's the title was
changed to "In an English Towne," sung by Marty Wilde and
later re-recorded by U.S. artist Chris Montez.

Rene Hall recalled how they had to do several takes of the
song because of the "awkward" metering of the piece. Said Hall,
"We had to follow Ritchie all the way through this number."

At first glance, one may think that there was little organiza-
tion to the rhythm of the piece, but the rather offbeat shifting of
meters is used very regularly in the vocal line (4/4–5/4–4/4, with
3/4 used in the refrain) and irregularly in the guitar solo (3/4–
5/4–3/4–4/4). Even with the guitar solo's irregularity, the 3/4
meter seems to hold it all together. The melodic phrase begins
on the third beat for both the vocal line and the guitar solo. As
for the melody, Ritchie sings within the limits of the I (tonic) and
IV (sub-dominant) chords, giving the illusion of an "oriental"
melody within a diatonic (seven-tone or major) scale. The guitar
solo further emphasizes that illusion by coming in with a melodic
line that virtually begins like a pentatonic (five-tone) scale! Only
when that line continues does it return to the diatonic or major
scale. It is as if Ritchie were actually *thinking* of a song of "oriental" origin! In addition, the guitar hyphens the melodic line of
the solo with straight amp vibrato.

As far as this writer knows, the shifting of meters and the
illusion of the use of scales other than the major or minor western scales was not approached deliberately in an original pop-
rock song until the time of the Beatles. It is curious and certainly
harmless to speculate about how Ritchie may have thought of the
idea of shifting meters, or about whether he was consciously
aware of the shifting. In other known recordings, Ritchie had
played in the basic 4/4 meter, shifting accents in the rhythmic
patterns. "Rockin' All Night" and "Rock Little Donna" are two
such examples. In Mexican folk music, it is quite common to shift
accents within a basic rhythmic pattern. Ritchie may have consciously thought of these shifting accents, but the final results
came out as the unique shifting of meters. Whatever the case
may be, "In a Turkish Town" may always remain a mystery as one
of the most complicated pieces of the 1950's.

The song, "Dooby Dooby Wah," billed in the promotional
sheet as the "finale" of the first album, was the b/w side for the

British release of "Come On, Let's Go" (Pye Int. 7N 25000), issued in October, 1958, as the first day of the Pye International Series). It was never released as a single in America. There is some documentation, however, in a Valens memorial booklet that was part of a limited series of Del-Fi EPs, that this was the "other song" besides "Ooh, My Head" intended for the Alan Freed movie *Go Johnny Go*. Speculation suggests that at some point and for some unknown reason the song was edited.

"Dooby Dooby Wah" is not a song that is well-remembered by the sessions musicians and outside of Ritchie possibly playing lead guitar and Palmer on the drums, the other musicians are not known for sure. The instrumentation is heavily guitar-oriented and some of the guitar playing may have been dubbed in after the initial session. It can be speculated that the instrumentation was as follows: lead guitar, possibly Valens; rhythm guitar, possibly two; dan-electro; stand-up bass; and drums, Palmer.

The writers of "Dooby Dooby Wah" are listed as Valens and "Kuhn," yet the song seems strikingly simple, almost too simple for two people to write. In all its essence, "Dooby Dooby Wah" seems to be mostly Valens—a type of song that may have been written on the spur of the moment. At first glance, the song could be considered anything but Valens' best, yet it contains all the elements of a good Valens rocker: strong use of sequential I, IV and V chords; use of nonsensical words, stressing the rhythmic qualities of the song, in other words, a good piece for dancing. There is, however, another hidden potential about "Dooby Dooby Wah." This selection has a strong "group" or "doo-wop" sound to it, along with a Latin tinge not unlike "Come On, Let's Go." There is a sustaining vocal line such as a lead singer would do in that style. In a way, it seems meant to have been sung by more than one person. After hearing this recording, to imagine one person singing "doo-wop" would possibly be to imagine Ritchie Valens! The predominance of guitars and off-beat syncopation of the bass (not unlike modern-day reggae!) add to the strength of the piece.

The nonsensical words, "dooby-dooby wah" are not far from a song released earlier in March, 1958, which began with the phrases, "doo run de run de run de papa,"—"I Met Him On A Sunday," the Shirelles first hit. Again, the use of "doo-wop" or a group song carried out by one solo singer—Ritchie.

7

The Stories Behind the Songs, III

"Ritchie"—The Songs

Following almost immediately on the heels of the first album titled *Ritchie Valens*, the second album, *Ritchie,* was released sometime during the early summer of 1959, because, according to several sources, the demand for more Valens recordings was intensified in the wake of his tragic demise. Several of the songs from this second album may possibly have been recorded in early January of that year, shortly before Ritchie left on the Winter Tour. Besides "Paddiwack Song" and "Little Girl" discussd earlier, they were: "Stay Beside Me," "Cry, Cry, Cry," "My Darling Is Gone," "Now You're Gone," "Hurry Up," "Rockin' All Night," and three instrumentals—"Big Baby Blues," "Fast Freight," and "Ritchie's Blues."

The first song on the album, "Stay Beside Me," is a far cry from the typical Valens style. Its rather saccharine lyrics echo songs sung in the early 60's by teenage celebrities of family TV shows, such as Shelley Fabares and Paul Peterson, "The Donna Reed Show"; and Johnny Crawford, "Rifleman," who ironically signed with Del-Fi and later recorded Valens' "Donna." "Stay Beside Me" was written by B. Olofson and M. Ellenhorn, on whom there is no information. Keane on the back of the album said that this song "reflects the lonely style," and L.A. writer Dawson called the song "a reflection of the Everly Brothers' style." Oddly enough, two of the sessions musicians also have kind words for the song. Hall called the piece "beautiful," and remembered that he was the one playing the sustaining guitar chords on the recording; Carol Kaye claimed that she played the rhythmic guitar pattern which connects the piece on the acoustic Epiphone Emperor guitar. She said, "It's a beautiful sounding rhythm. I still have the guitar [used on the song]." Ironically, this piece is more harmonically complicated than the typical Valens selections of I, IV and V, with sequences going into minor and even diminished guitar chords. However, the rhythmic guitar pattern Kaye played is also associated with Valens' style of playing, especially in "Donna." The suspicion that Ritchie may also be playing the rhythmic pattern cannot be overlooked. There is only one rhythmic pattern and the sustaining guitar chords are played by Hall. They serve as the "lead" in the piece. It is also possible that Kaye's playing may have been dubbed over Ritchie's. The other sessions musician, namely the bass player, is not known.

"Stay Beside Me" was released as a single (DF 4128) in October, 1959, and virtually went nowhere, as it was not the custom at the time to push songs of deceased rock performers. Though this song could be classified as the soft style associated with Valens' ballads, it is far from being Valens' best. The soulful touch he employed in most of his slow songs is sorely lacking in this piece.

The second song in the album is titled "Cry, Cry, Cry." The title name has been used in two other recordings, although there is no connection to Johnny Cash's "Cry, Cry, Cry" nor Bobby "Blue" Bland's recording. This was the last Del-Fi single release of Ritchie Valens, the b/w side being "Paddiwack Song" (DF 4133); it was released in mid-1960, with little or no results. "Cry, Cry, Cry" was also cowritten with "Kuhn."

Outside of Valens, who plays the leading guitar riff and break, and Palmer who plays the drums, the other sessions musicians may have been Hall on dan-electro or rhythm, Kaye on dan-electro or rhythm and Clarke or Pitman on the bass. Apparently, the song has no special origin although it bears a slight resemblance in melody to the Penguins' "Hey, Señorita," the b/w side of their classic hit of 1954, "Earth / Angel." Curiously enough, a latter-day Beatle tune, "Birthday," bears a guitar riff and even a word arrangement similar to "Cry, Cry, Cry," although this may be sheer coincidence.

The guitar riff in "Cry, Cry, Cry" is the key to the whole piece. The rhythm of it is typically "Valens," that is, it carries virtually the same rhythmic pattern as "That's My Little Suzie," "Dooby Dooby Wah" and some of the incomplete fragments.

The rhythmic pattern used in "Cry, Cry, Cry" is: ♩♩♪ ♫ ♩♩ ♩♩ | ♪___etc., while "Suzie" is: ♩♩♪ ♫ ♪♪♪ ♪♪♪ The basic ♩♩♪ ♫ ♩♩ ♩ etc. is quite typical of many Valens rockers. Another interesting factor about the guitar riff is that it is being played in a strict major scale while Valens is singing flat 3rds in a basic twelve-bar blues progression. Also, the dropping of the voice at the end of each phrase is quite typical and the way Ritchie stresses the word "come" is most noteworthy. So many elements have gone into "Cry, Cry, Cry" that it expresses the height of a Valens rocker more than possibly any other song outside of "La Bamba."

Two ballads that appear on the second album, accompanied only with guitar and vocal, were probably recorded at Keane's home as demos. One of them, "My Darling Is Gone," (actually, Ritchie sings "My Darlin's Gone" on the recording) is Ritchie's own composition played on an amplified acoustic guitar and strummed in 6/8 time in the style of "Stay Beside Me" and "Donna." "My Darling Is Gone" is referred to as being on the same line as "Donna," but the song is more simplified, more "folkish" in quality, with a guitar break at the end of each phrase and the words, being more prosaic than rhythmic, seem to have been made up as the song was recorded. Little is known about this song except that the melody may have an origin in a 1957 tune "I Love You So," the flip side of the hit "Gee" by the Crows.

In the recording, one can actually hear "movement" while the song is going on. There is a particularly noticeable sound, similar to the rocking of a chair. According to several sources, it was said that Ritchie liked to sit in the rocking chair in Keane's home, while singing and strumming his guitar.

"My Darling Is Gone" is meant to be quiet and reflective, from the simple guitar strumming (with the following rhythm: ⁶⁄₈ ♩♫ ♩ ♫♩ which is also used in most Valens ballads) to simple choral harmonies of I, IV, V (with an occasional use of the dominant, i.e., V of V). Its simpleness has the pure essence of Ritchie's vocal quality and especially of his discernible high tenor.

Almost the same could be said for another ballad on the album "Now You're Gone," with one noticeable difference: the employment of an electrical guitar and possibly the one Ritchie originally owned, the Sears Stratotone. Because of this differ-

ence, "Now You're Gone" sounds more amplified, less serene
than "My Darling Is Gone." Even though the strumming technique is the same and the harmonies are very similar, Ritchie's
vocal and guitar are consistent with each other in being more
forceful and pronounced. Perhaps, the more intense feeling of
"Now You're Gone" was intentional. Again, there is the influence
of "I Love You So," but there is more of a feeling for the "doo-
wop" sound than in "My Darling Is Gone." Ritchie does impres-
sive crescendos with his voice, worthy of the tradition of a lead in
"doo-wop." There is, however, a slight weakness in the uneven
use of an echo chamber. Also, Ritchie essentially lacks the high
falsetto needed to sing the "oos" associated with "doo-wop" music.

Another interesting factor that makes "Now You're Gone"
quite different is that it is virtually a *through-composed* song. In
other words, the words are non-rhymic and the melodic verses
are similar but different. The *through-composed* form of this piece
would be: A, A¹, A², B, A³ Coda. Generally speaking, this song
remains more complicated than what is superficially heard and
Ritchie's spontaneity has to be admired regarding this selection.
In light of what has been said about "Now You're Gone" and "My
Darling Is Gone," they might be called "peripheral songs," that
is, songs that relate to an earlier and more "major" song. In this
case, it would be "Donna," for these pieces apparently came at
the same time. Many of "Donna's" phrases and the theme of a
guy breaking up with his girlfriend are echoed in the other two
songs. The melancholy phrase of the guy who "does not know
what to do, now that she's gone" brings all three of these songs
together.

The last song on the "A" side of *Ritchie*, "Hurry Up," is
somewhat of a novelty song. Though a good rocker, it is another
example of a song a little out of the ordinary for Valens, perhaps
in respect to who composed it.

The composer of "Hurry Up" was none other than Sharon
Sheeley, then fiancée of Eddie Cochran. She and Eddie met
Ritchie for the first time at the Alan Freed Christmas show in
December, 1958. They rapidly became friends and spent most of
the Christmas holiday together. "I wrote 'Hurry Up' when I was
waiting for Eddie," said Sheeley. "He was always very late,
whooping it up with Johnny Burnette and I was sitting there.
Eddie kept calling me saying, 'Honey, I'll be there in another

hour, I'm still in the traffic on the freeway,' or 'I'll be another hour.' During one three-hour period waiting to go to the movies, I wrote '*Hurry Up*, or I'll get another date' which is how the lyrics went. Then, when Eddie finally came, I showed him the little song and he said, 'That's great for Ritchie. So, Eddie went in and made a demo for Ritchie, which Ritchie recorded." However, Sheeley said that she never had the demo returned nor received royalties for the song. She added, "Mr. Keane sort of had an amazing way of making everybody's royalties disappear real quickly."

"Hurry Up" was known to have been recorded in early January, 1959, but the instrumentation of the song and who played it are in question. Outside of Valens on vocal and guitar (lead or rhythm is not known), Buddy Clarke on upright bass and Palmer on drums, there are possibly one or two other guitars in the piece. The background vocals and the clapping may have been dubbed in later, and the people responsible for these added touches remain a mystery. It is known that Keane did not hire extra background singers and the voices may have been his, Ritchie's or other musicians.

There is a definite sense that Ritchie enjoyed singing "Hurry Up," displaying a strong yet teasing anger in his vocal expression. The words are slurred a little bit to add to the current emotion of the song. In addition to "Little Girl," this is another song Ritchie modulates from one key to the next (E to F). Finally, the guitar parts interlock with each other in an almost "Latin" feel, while the drums maintain a basic rock and roll rhythm.

"Rockin' All Night," the last song on the *Ritchie* album, may have also been a demo. It contains just Ritchie singing and playing and a mysterious vocal backdrop of "Ba doo wa sha bops," which may have belonged to Keane or the musicians. On the cover notes Keane stated that "Rockin' All Night" "demonstrated Ritchie's style as a really exciting rock and roll singer and is a perfect example of how he composed the song as he sang it, with never a wrong word or a bad note."

Of all the Valens songs, "Rockin' All Night" is the most imitative of the rockabilly style. The guitar breaks are mostly in the tradition of Chuck Berry (with an occasional Valens riff thrown in), and the vocal inflections echo more of Elvis and, to a lesser extent, Eddie Cochran, even to the point of masking the regular Valens vocal quality! This song can be likened to "Rock Little

Donna" in that the words are made up as the song progresses. Curiously, the words of the song seem more "suggestive," very unlike the "innocence" of most Valens tunes. "Kiss me all night long," as implied in "Rockin' All Night," suggests more than just dancing all night to the rhythm of a good beat! The guitar passages are improvisational, and most noteworthy is the ending, a prolonged guitar chord, with an upbeat. Yet, there is serious question as to whether this song can be considered a "best" for the Valens style. It is common rockabilly and strongly imitative. Bob Morales had a strong comment to make concerning Ritchie's imitations of Berry or Elvis, which related particularly to this selection: "That's the one thing I used to tell Ritchie—'Hang up that kind of playing and get into you, man! Leave Elvis and Chuck Berry to Elvis and Chuck Berry.'" Despite its excitement as a good rock and roll tune, "Rockin' All Night" falls short of innovation in the Valens repertoire.

"Ritchie"—The Instrumentals

Two of the instrumentals on the second album, "Big Baby Blues" b/w "Fast Freight," were previously released on a single (DF 4111), approximately around the same time as "Donna." However, they were titled under the anagram of "Arvee Allens" (i.e., R.V. Allens = R. Valens). Both instrumentals were short one-take jam sessions that sounded well enough to Keane for releases. Theoretically, Keane was hoping to find another market for Ritchie's talents should his vocal discs fail or as British writer Simon Philips put it, "if white America was put off by his distinct Chicano accent or by the complete Spanish sound and lyrics of 'La Bamba.'" The disc failed on the music charts even though the single was reviewed in *Billboard* with good kudos. Initially, there was no reference to Valens being related to "Arvee Allens," but ironically, once it was known that "Allens" was in fact, Valens, the record did get a little airplay, especially in the wake of the tragedy.

Probably the most unique concept about both "Big Baby Blues" and "Fast Freight" was the special use of jazz improvisation on a rock instrumental. This idea was hardly explored until the mid-60's with the "official" beginnings of jazz-rock fusion. Buddy Clarke was already one of the top jazz bassists and a major influence behind this sound, as was Earl Palmer who employed some of the drum techniques used in the r 'n' b New Orleans sessions of Fats Domino, Little Richard and Roy Brown. Dawson called this combination of established professional Black musicians with an upcoming Chicano musician "a special sound unlike any other."

The instrumentation on both selections is as follows: lead guitar (Valens); dan-electro (possibly Hall or Pitman); stand-up bass (Clarke); rhythm guitar (possibly Kaye); and drums (Palmer). "Big Baby Blues," only one minute and forty-five seconds long, has the feel of an "overtime" piece often played by blues bands as an introduction or intermission break during a performance, and therefore seems more commonplace nowadays than it may have seemed at the time. This recording gives a special insight into the knowledge Ritchie may have had of blues. It is ironic that Bo Diddley, one of the founding fathers of early rock, once said that improvisations played on blues guitar should be slow and not in the running-note style that is characteristic of B.B. King, which Diddley felt most white rock musicians emulated. It is interesting to know that in this selection, with the exception of one spot, Ritchie plays that traditionally slow improvisational style that Diddley emphasized.

"Fast Freight," a one-take jam session lasting one minute and fifty-two seconds, is far more eclectic than "Big Baby Blues" and is the model of early jazz-rock fusion. Several of the guitar licks in this piece may have also been influenced by Eddie Cochran. The addition of Clarke's special bass improvisation and Palmer's drum technique is worthy of Keane's statement on the back of the second album: "'Fast Freight' shows [Valens'] great prowess on the guitar, and tells the rocking story of a fast freight charging through the night." The railroad tracks of the northern Valley area of Pacoima and San Fernando dominated the sounds of the environment surrounding Valens as he was growing up. This instrumental carries the standard blues progression with a sense of a five-tone pentatonic melody, adding the strong downbeat in one musical phrase and a lighter upbeat in the next, a unique Valens quality found also in incomplete fragments. There is also one tiny segment where Ritchie uses a pencil (possibly the lead end of it) to pick a note or two, a technique he later employed more profusely in another instrumental, "Ritchie's Blues."

One of the most interesting facets of "Fast Freight" is its highly unusual and programmatic ending, in which Ritchie and the other guitarists, to indicate the halting of the "train," play notes on the guitar as if they were "scattered" in all directions. This "note-breaking" technique Keane called, "a lot of mistakes, that we faded out early to get out." In certain re-releases of this song on later LPs, the ending is totally omitted. Dawson called this fantastic finale, "a psychedelic vibrato fadeout." The likes of such an ending was not found again in rock music until the late 60's! "Fast Freight" is truly one of the most rocking, driving instrumentals of the late fifties, using musical sounds not previously explored in great depths.

The final instrumental on the album, "Ritchie's Blues," was a test that was later taken into the studios in order to dub in the percussion. It was a one-take session that was probably not meant for commercial release. This instrumental can be considered one of Valens' most eclectic musical pieces, with a mystery as veiled as "In a Turkish Town." "Ritchie's Blues" contains all the elements stated by writer Dawson: "Besides being the first distinctly California rocker, Valens would have been the first to create an African/European/Latin hybrid of rock." The piece has an unusual treatment of the twelve-bar blues and a very subdued Latin beat in the form of a chalypso played by the percussion. But the rhythmic aspects of the guitar are distinctly Afro-Hispanic, using much vibrato technique. The melodic line stresses strong fourth and fifth intervals.

The guitar is played mostly with a pick until the end, where there is use of a pencil as the pick. For "Ritchie's Blues," it is possible that both ends of the pencil were used, although no one now really knows how Ritchie employed that technique. Had Ritchie lived, it would be hard to speculate if "Ritchie's Blues" would have still been a part of the second album. We can only speculate about whether the development of the pencil-picking idea would have been carried out in other Valens' compositions.

"Ritchie Valens in Concert at Pacoima Junior High"—The Concert

The event that led to the release of a third album in early 1960 was a morning assembly around 10:00 A.M. at Pacoima Junior High in early December, 1958. Ritchie, now a well known rock artist, was the featured act. The junior high school newspaper, *The Torch*, announced that the assembly was to be scheduled for Friday, December 5th, but somehow, because of Ritchie's busy schedule, the concert was postponed until the following Wednesday, December 10th.

Gail Smith, a student at Pacoima Junior High and also the L.A. president of the Ritchie Valens Fan Club, said, "I got the idea of doing the assembly in order to sell subscriptions to the junior high school annual. The principal had recorded the assembly over the P.A. system, then he gave me the tape. When Ritchie was killed and Bob (Keane) didn't have any more material, he asked me if he could do the album. I let him take the tape and he cut out what he wanted." There is much distortion, especially because of the screams and other audience responses. (Between the selections, one can hear fragments of audience response. It may be that parts of the assembly not directly pertinent to Valens were omitted.) Keane nonetheless felt that the concert was audible enough to be released alongside "Malagueña" and some other incomplete songs and instrumentals Ritchie had composed.

The concert portion of the album is special in itself because it is one of the few rock 'n' roll concerts from the late 50's recorded live of a single rock 'n' roll performer and practically the only surviving entity in which Ritchie is interviewed.

The album is narrated by Bob Keane, with his introductory remarks also printed on the back of the album cover. The concert begins with a nervous introduction by Gail Smith. Ritchie then proceeds to sing "Come On, Let's Go," the alternate version, even though his drummer, Don Philips, doesn't accompany him. Philips then joins Ritchie, who sings "Donna," which differs only slightly in the beginning chordal progression from the commercial recording (I, II, IV, V). Smith then requests Ritchie to do the Eddie Cochran standard "Summertime Blues," made famous in August of that year. Just before he starts playing, Ritchie says while adjusting his guitar, "Let's see if I can have a little bit more volume . . . getting old!"

What Valens produces is a version unlike the uptempo rhythm of Cochran's but, as writer Bangs put it, "a sound as if it was written for him." The tempo is slower but not dragging; the approach can be described as more "sensuous" than "energetic." The tuning at the beginning of the piece lends a slightly "pentatonic" sound, a riff later used in other instrumentals and the fragments.

What follows is Smith's introduction to an instrumental Ritchie had recently composed, "From Beyond":

SMITH: "He just wrote this. They were just fiddlin' around."

VALENS: "This is a song which you call was made in one day. I know it's not the wildest but we're going to try it out, okay? (Pause) Then, we have "From Right Beyond!" (Away from mike) Here we go!"

Keane referred to the melody of the instrumental as "melancholy," with a "sense of inherent sadness . . . kind of a dirge." The twanginess of the guitar echoes an obvious Duane Eddy influence, and the musical motive found in the tune-up at the beginning of "Summertime Blues" is well inserted into this instrumental. Philips' drumming slightly suggests some of the basic rhythms that were later used in surfer music of the early 60's, especially in the slower "surf" songs.

The last part of the concert consisted of a short interview in which Ritchie talked about his trip to Hawaii and the TV shows and other shows he would appear on around town. The final tune of the assembly is "La Bamba," which is played slower and in pace with the drummer. Ritchie's strumming is similar to the riffs used on "Rock Little Donna" and the earlier rendition of "Come On, Let's Go." His singing seems more like "shouting," although this may be due to the distortion of the mike.

As mentioned before, there were other parts of the assembly that seem like "gaps" on the recording. According to Smith, all the songs Ritchie sang in the concert were not included in the album, although Smith cannot remember which ones were omitted. Also, a local duo, John and Judy Maus, performed at this concert. (John went on to become part of the Walker Brothers, a popular British group during the mid and late 60's.) There may have been other portions in which Ritchie was interviewed which were not recorded. A picture exists that indicates that a drawing took place, since the picture shows Ritchie choosing the winner, while two girls, Gail and Judy look on. Said Smith, "Just about the whole school had turned out for the one-hour assembly."

"Malagueña"

Probably the most profound selection to emerge from the Pacoima Junior High School album had nothing to do with the assembly. One of the demo pieces placed on the second side of the album, "Malagueña," was originally recorded at the home of Bob Keane. Keane, in his narration, called the instrumental "a great Mexican standard" to which Ritchie planned to add a set of American love lyrics. Dawson called the piece another example of the "African/European/Latin hybrid of rock . . . a song rare and familiar to few record collectors and is perhaps the guide-post for determining Valens' direction." However, the background of "Malagueña" and Ritchie's relationship to it was never fully explored until now.

What Ritchie played in his interpretation of "Malagueña" was not one but *two* different pieces of music. Though both were popular in Mexican circles, their origins were more Spanish and only one of them could be classified as a *malagueña* (originally a variant of a flamenco song from the city of Málaga in southern Spain).

The predominant song of Ritchie's interpretation is "España Cani," a *pasodoble* or march often heard at bullfights and origin-ally written in 1934 by a Spaniard, Pascual Marquina; the major melody in the middle of the piece is Ernesto Lecuona's "Mala-gueña," written in the 1930's by a Cuban bandleader who also wrote classical piano pieces with a Spanish/flamenco flavor.

An interesting point about "España Cani" is that the misno-mer of the song as a "malagueña" goes beyond the album notes of Ritchie Valens. Apparently, many guitarists, Hispanic or oth-erwise, have mistaken the song as such and the reason is quite understandable. In their primary melodies, both Lecuona's "Ma-lagueña" and Marquina's "España Cani" stress the following chordal progressions: Em, F, G, F sharp, F, Em in the Phrygian scale. This chordal progression is typical of *malagueñas* and other flamenco music. "España Cani" begins this way, so theoretically (and in Valens' case, applicably), that song could easily be merged with Lecuona's "Malagueña" into one musical improvi-sation.

The idea that Keane presented for Ritchie's "Malagueña" to be made into a vocal piece would have been very unique since neither Lecuona's nor Marquina's compositions originally had lyrics. Perhaps Ritchie would have set words to his interpreta-tion. Or perhaps Ritchie would have sung yet *another* "mala-gueña," "La Malagueña Salerosa," a popular Mexican folk song from the *huasteca* region which has little to do with the Spanish *malagueña*. The melody of the piece does not appear at all in any of Ritchie's songs, yet it is known that he knew some of the words to "Salerosa." Young Chicanos who play guitar would normally learn Lecuona's version and "Salerosa" because, as one L.A. professional guitarist put it, "at family gatherings, they would want to hear both." There is no known recording of Ritchie singing "Salerosa," so the possibility of his adding English lyrics to it or to the already existing instrumental will forever remain pure speculation.

Ritchie played his improvisation of "Malagueña" in the key of F, either tuned up a half-step or capoed up the first fret because the tonal center of the Phrygian mode is the key of E. One particular riff using ascending parallel fourth chords, common in other Valens fragments, is noted in examining how Ritchie approached the particular mode of the piece. In that mode, one would normally go up E, F, G, but Ritchie went E, F sharp, G sharp—instead of half-steps typical of the original mode, Ritchie took whole steps!

Ritchie's eclectic interpretation of "Malagueña" has to be considered a complete work in itself, pure Ritchie Valens without the sessions musicians or overdubbing. For that, "Malagueña" is not only a diversion from the rock 'n' roll of the late 50's, it is also quite a diversion from what Valens normally produced in his hit recordings. The most surprising factor about this selection is how much was picked up by a young boy who had virtually no formal guitar training. Considering the time period, location and exposure, Ritchie Valens' "Malagueña" is indeed an amazing feat for a young man.

The Fragments

Ideas not polished or songs considered incomplete by commercial standards comprised the second side of the Pacoima Junior High School album. These selections, including "Malagueña," were probably recorded in Keane's basement studio and were possibly done around early January, 1959. Supposedly, these musical ideas Ritchie was planning to develop once he returned from the "Winter Dance Party" tour.

The first throwaway track, titled "Rhythm Song," is an instrumental that may or may not have been considered a candidate for later lyrics. Nevertheless, it works well as merely an instrumental. Bangs in 1970 said, "[Rhythm Song] reveals strong strains from the Pop Staples school of funky bass-strings reverb guitar playing." Beyond being simply a "throwaway track," this short selection is similar to the instrumental "From Beyond" in that it hints at the earliest beginnings of what was later to be "surf music." This is *not* to say that Ritchie Valens was in any way directly responsible for surf music, and both Keane and Hall flatly deny that connection. But it cannot be overlooked that Ritchie may have been *exposed* to Dick Dale, who was later called "The King of Surf Music."

Bob Keane was Dale's first manager, before Dale developed the "surf" beat, and before Ritchie signed up with Keane. In an article, Dale said, "I tutored both Cochran and Valens. They both appeared with me at the Long Beach Auditorium." What Dale and subsequently those who followed him played were expressions of the garage-band sounds that developed out of the *coastal* suburbs of L.A. and southern California; what Ritchie played developed from the San Fernando Valley area and especially the northern section. This "Rhythm Song" shows the meeting of the two experiences, in addition to the musical influences of Bo Diddley, who, in essence, has been considered by many rock enthusiasts as the "ultimate originator" of surf music!

There is another connection, though indirect, between the surf style and Ritchie Valens—the appearance of the Beach Boys in their first major concert two years later, New Year's Eve, 1961, at the Ritchie Valens Memorial Dance, yet there is no evidence that the Valens sound affected the Beach Boys' music in any way.

Another way "Rhythm Song" is similar to "From Beyond" is in Ritchie's use of the familiar pentatonic guitar riff to build up an improvisation based mostly on Berry riffs. This pentatonic riff (which also appears in "Summertime Blues" and the commercially recorded "Fast Freight") is *exactly* the same as a guitar riff used at the beginning of an Eric Clapton 1976 song called "Layla." Clapton plays this riff at a much faster tempo than Valens ever did, *yet it is the same riff*. Since it is not known where Ritchie may have picked up this particular riff, it seems likely that this riff may be an original.

The second track, simply called "Guitar Instrumental" shows, as Keane points out in his narration, the influence of Bo Diddley. Both did appear on the same bill, the Alan Freed Christmas show of 1958. Diddley had the following to say about Valens:

"I'm very happy that I was an influence on [Valens] music. He was a pretty neat dude but anything he picked up from me, he was probably eyeballing me and got it that way. As far as myself sitting down and showing somebody something, that didn't happen."

The melody is essentially pentatonic, with certain patterns played twice, first in the lower register of the guitar, then on the upper register, creating what is known as a "call and response" musical pattern, strongly evocative of the musical essence of the Black American tradition. Because of this pattern, the melody line is very song-like, even though Ritchie may not have been thinking of a song at the time. The use of the familiar parallel fourth chords found in "Malagueña" breaks the continuity of the five-tone melody with its more "major scale" sound.

After the selection of "Malagueña" on the album, comes a short piece Ritchie composed, for which the words are written on the back of the album. "Rock Little Darlin'" is about, as Keane described it, "a boy who loved to dance." Ritchie combines hard and soft strumming as well as the basic 4/4 rhythmic pattern characterized in several Valens rockers. The song is extremely topical, repeating the melody but using different words, an element which may imply what the game song "Mama Long" may have been like. The last line of the verse (not printed on the back of the cover) is somewhat indiscernible but may be "dance our troubles away."

The last fragment called "Let's Rock 'n' Roll" has the same strumming techniques as "Rock Little Darlin'." Keane called it "another 'Come On, Let's Go'"; actually, it is very much like "Rockin' All Night," without the vocal backup. The biggest difference between the two songs is that Ritchie sounds more like himself in "Let's Rock 'n' Roll." There is a use of flat third chords as in "Rock Little Donna" and the tempo is slower than most Valens rockers but the most interesting part of the song is the very beginning where Ritchie uses a vocal slide upward, something not found in any of his other pieces. Again, the words seem as if they were created spontaneously.

Are There Any Other Fragments?

Within the last few years, a Ritchie Valens discography appeared in a German fanzine, listing, of all things, seven musical selections reputed to have been released in both Europe (especially France) and Australia, heretofore unknown. They were as follows:

> "Bridge of Sighs" / "Scene of a Crime"
> (45-single—Vogue/Coral Label [France])
>
> An LP on the Festival (Australia) label:
> "Bwana Niña" (Pretty Girl)
> "Sixteen Candles"
> (Two unknown pieces—instrumentals?)
>
> (There is also believed to exist a twelve-minute studio version of "Ooh, My Head" described in the discography as "demoband vom 13.5.58," meaning it was recorded May 13, 1958. It is not known whether this recording is on a recording disc.)

To this date, there is little indication that these selections are *bona-fide* Ritchie Valens releases. Yet, there is little proof that they are *not*. If, in any way, they are authentic Valens releases, the names were obviously tagged onto the pieces at a much later date, for titles such as "Bridge of Sighs" and "Scene of a Crime" and the pseudo-Swahili/Latin name "Bwana Niña" were virtually non-existent in the 50's. "Scene of a Crime" may have been an alternate take of "Framed," while "Bwana Niña" may be another version of "Boney-Maronie." The title "Bridge of Sighs" is rather puzzling. However, the possibility of Ritchie singing a version of the Crests' "Sixteen Candles" is highly likely. According to Mrs. Reyes, Ritchie did associate with the members of that group during the Christmas show, as was mentioned earlier in describing their bet on whose hit would reach No. 1 first.

The twelve-minute version of "Oh, My Head" and the two unknown pieces on the lost Australian LP are likely possibilities confirmed by both the Reyes and by Bob Keane. Mrs. Reyes said, "Keane has the only tape left over from the songs Ritchie had written. There were songs he had written here in this house and not *all* of them appeared on the Pacoima album." She also recalled a time she and her husband went to Del-Fi studios to hear some songs that were yet to be released.

Keane on the other hand said, "I've got a lot of work tapes because I worked out of my home a lot. I've got quite a few tapes where Ritchie's trying out things and talking. But I don't feel there'll be much interest in that (kind of thing) with just Ritchie."

Whether some of these tapes may have found their way out

of the Del-Fi spectrum (as in the case of "Rock Little Donna" on Guest Star) or are still within the confines of Keane's property is uncertain. In what *condition* these tapes may be is another matter. For a recent release of Valens recordings through Rhino Records in July, 1981, the following was printed in the pamphlet of the three-record box set: ". . . many of the original tapes were lost and had to be reconstructed from the best original discs . . ." Also, several of the original tapes had deteriorated over the period of time. That could also be true of any of the other tapes Keane might possess.

In addition to the work tapes described by both Keane and Mrs. Reyes, there is also the controversial Silhouettes tape Macchia gave to Keane before the audition. There is also another Silhouettes tape in the possession of Bill Jones, which may or may not be of top quality. Other speculations include Louis Raring's report that one of the private parties Ritchie performed at was taped, as well as Donna Fox's recollection of a possible taping of one of Ritchie's performances at San Fernando High. There is even a rumor of a taped concert in Honolulu, Hawaii! These last three possibilities have been explored and, to date, nothing has been found.

There was supposed to have been an accounting of all Valens material in 1985, but nothing has come of it to date. With the release of the upcoming film, more material not previously known may at last come into the open once the rights to the Valens material have been established.

8

THE MAKING OF A
ROCK AND ROLL STAR

Shows Around the Country

Sometime around August, 1958, Bob Keane began promoting "Come On, Let's Go," by approaching KFWB. This L.A. based radio station was the AM powerhouse of the top forty hits and a guarantee for any song played, a chance for hitdom. As Bill Angel, former music director of KFWB, put it, "Anything we got on, people just ran and bought." Chuck Blore, KFWB program director, had previously known Keane via Sam Cooke so there was little problem in getting "Come On, Let's Go" airplay. Angel recalled that the KFWB disc jockeys favored Ritchie's personality, something that seldom occurred with a beginning rock performer, and they were willing to assist him in any way. On one occasion, D.J. Elliot Field set up an interview with Ritchie and some high school students. But it was Ted Quillin who befriended Ritchie the most. From the beginning, Ritchie used to visit Quillin's all-night show and talk about various subjects, including music.

Quillin saw Ritchie as a youngster who held the whole phenomenon of a rock star's popularity in awe. Ritchie found it hard to believe that it was happening to him, yet his cautiousness, as well as his confidence, was building. Quillin related how secure Ritchie felt about discussing basic show business problems with him and also that Ritchie did not hesitate to seek his assistance on certain legal and financial matters. Not fully aware of the complexities of show business arrangements, Ritchie found an honest friend in Quillin, someone who was not attempting to make a buck off him. Ritchie would always inquire about certain local appearances they would do, later asking Quillin, "How's it sound to you?" At the height of "Donna/La Bamba," Quillin remembered saying to Ritchie, "Hey, you gotta watch 'cause everybody in town is trying to blow your ass full of smoke and dazzle you with footwork and let you know it's 'Hollywood.' Don't loose touch, man!"

"We had a groovy relationship," said Quillin. "I was like a big brother to him. We talked about different stars—Ray Charles, Bobby 'Blue' Bland, Bo Diddley, Chuck Berry, Jerry Lee Lewis—oh, he loved Jerry Lee Lewis! That wasn't his particular [performing] style, but he could dig it." One song Quillin remembered as Ritchie's favorite was the Diamonds' "Little Darlin'." Concerning Ritchie's own performing style, Quillin said, "He had the excitement, the drive. He had that extra help of enthusiasm, plus he was good. If he had lived, there would've been no Trini López, 'cause he could burn him down! Ritchie had a great earthiness about him. He wasn't trying to do something he couldn't do. He was doing what he knew."

Besides the all-night show and the local hops featuring guest artists, Ritchie also participated with Quillin in "Oh Boy, Pizza" contests in which the winners would get an evening with Ritchie Valens at their home. This happened especially when "Donna/La Bamba" was high on the charts. In addition to the KFWB promoted hops, Ritchie also appeared on local TV dance shows sponsored by D.J.'s such as Al Jarvis, "Jolly" Joe Yokum, Earl McDaniels and Art Laboe.

By September, 1958, "Come On, Let's Go" started making the national charts and Keane decided on a nationwide promotion, travelling the circuit on the road. During the latter part of that month, and into October, manager and performer travelled up and down the East Coast to eleven cities in ten days. It was on October 6th, Ritchie's mother's birthday, that he first appeared on "American Bandstand" in Philadelphia to sing "Come On, Let's Go." It was also on this very same show that Dick Clark asked Ritchie to make up a song about Clark, which he did. Ritchie also appeared on Alan Freed's TV show in New York, "The Buddy Deane Show" in Baltimore, Maryland and "The Milt Grant Show" in Washington, D.C. He may have also appeared at a local show in Chicago since two Chicago distribution agents by the names of Paul Glass and Earl Glicken helped promote sales for Del-Fi releases around that time. Ritchie may have also appeared in Buffalo, New York and possibly Toronto, Canada. The other five cities Ritchie performed in on this "tour" are not known. Keane could not recall which cities they were. However, the two also drove up to San Francisco for a local TV appearance there. While there, Keane bought a '59 silver-blue Thunderbird to drive back to Los Angeles.

It was sometime around late October, if not early November, that "Donna/La Bamba" was released. Not long afterward, engagements became more demanding within the Southern California area, with recurring appearances for Ritchie at Pacific Ocean Park, El Monte Legion Stadium, Long Beach Municipal Civic Auditorium, Harmony Park Ballroom, Ted Randel's, and Disneyland. Occasional appearances closer to home in the San Fernando Valley area never ceased.

All along, the Valley had recognized Ritchie as a popular figure, but the release of "Donna/La Bamba" once and for all established Ritchie Valens as a household name. The Silhouettes, Ritchie's former group, continued to play around the local area and on rare occasions, Ritchie and the group came together to perform. Most of the members understood Ritchie's new obligations, though they found his popularity a curiosity. Takaki recalled, "Even when Ritchie made 'Come On, Let's Go,' boy, you see all these people trying to get to him and hang around him. He had a whole bunch of guys coming after him that just wanted to do things for him. They kind of spoiled Ritchie in a way. His days was just filled with guys and girls. Ritchie had a hard time handling things like that but he didn't get annoyed 'cause this was something that was still new to him and he liked it. But it did give him a sense of power. He didn't know that but that's a change I really saw in him. With me, Gil and the rest of us, he was still the same Ritchie." Other close friends saw virtually no personality changes in Ritchie. "There was absolutely no personality change," said Mrs. Beckett, who saw Ritchie for the last time at the Long Beach Civic. "He treated me like he always treated me. It didn't matter that he was a big star or his name was up in lights. He came over to us, shook my brother's hand [Gil Rocha] and my hand and was so happy to see us." Boyhood friend Chaubet felt the same way, although he recalled an incident in which some girls who had previously shunned Ritchie because of his weight tried to get close to him now that he was popular. Ritchie reacted with a frank rebuttal. According to Chaubet, "His reaction was, 'You treated me badly but now that I got it made you wanted to be my friend, but that ain't gonna work. You can buy my records, but don't be my friend 'cause you ain't.' I thought it was funny myself." Judy Hoyt of the John and Judy duo recalls, "Ritchie was *very* helpful to us. Most people were not that sweet because it was competition or something. He really liked us and we liked him. My brother and I would play his records before we went on a show, because we thought it brought us good luck. We also used to sing 'In A Turkish Town' and 'La Bamba.'"

There is little indication that Ritchie's personality included pretentiousness even with strangers. One of the winners of the KFWB "Oh Boy, Pizza" contest, Bonnie Nash, recalled that Ritchie behaved "as if we had known him all through school," with a concern and excitement as tremendous as her own and her friends who attended the party. There was still another event remembered by Ritchie's aunt, which happened on Halloween in 1958. At the time, Ritchie was staying with her, giving him the opportunity to practice more often and in privacy, for later that evening, he had an engagement at a private party at Gail Smith's home. Mrs. Reyes had returned home from work when some children in their pre- and early teens came by to "trick or treat." She recalled, "I had just got home from work and hadn't run to the store. So I said to them, 'I don't have candy, but say, I'll tell you what. I'll give you a treat. You can listen to Ritchie Valens.' 'Who?! Ritchie Valens!' And they threw their trick or treat candy bags all over my front yard! Those kids were just tickled that he sang for them. He was barely getting started but I guess these kids knew who he was. They really got a treat that time."

From the Local Shows to the Alan Freed Christmas Show

New horizons awaited Ritchie, yet he never forgot his hometown acquaintances and school friends. Though he had dropped out of San Fernando High by early October, 1958, he did return to perform for a function put on by the Saracens, the senior high school class of that year, to benefit the new school board. Very little is known about that performance or on what date it occurred, although there is a photo of the performance in the 1959 school yearbook.

The showmanship that Ritchie displayed while performing with the Silhouettes persisted even after his recordings became

popular. Aside from the eventful "Boney-Maronie" performance at El Monte, one would have normally seen Ritchie standing perfectly still on stage, even when performing rockers, with
feet apart, occasionally tapping one foot to the rhythm of the
song and occasionally walking in a natural way from one side of
the stage to the next, depending where the microphone was set.
Ritchie never moved like other rock guitarists such as Chuck
Berry, Bo Diddley, and Eddie Cochran who gyrated or danced
with the guitar, even though such performers were often admired by him.

At the concert at Pacoima Junior High, Ritchie revealed that
he had just returned from a two-week engagement in Honolulu.
Keane disclaimed knowing anything about this trip: "He may
have gone to Hawaii by himself, but I did not go with him. I
know I was not involved with that." There is good speculation,
however, that Ritchie performed at the Honolulu Civic Auditorium under the "Show of Stars" promoted by Ralph Yempuku
and Earl Finch, who began producing rock 'n' roll shows earlier
that year for the Islands' enthusiasts. The first of these shows
starred Buddy Holly and the Crickets and Paul Anka, among
others.

Shortly after the December 10th Pacoima assembly, Ritchie
and his manager made their way to New York for the Alan Freed
Christmas show which began Christmas week, 1958, and ran
through the New Year's weekend of 1959. Tabbed as "Alan
Freed's Christmas Jubilee," it played at the old Loew's State
Theater and featured acts such as Johnny Ray (who was booted
from the show after a few days, apparently because he was too
"pop" for the mostly youthful audiences), the Everly Brothers,
Chuck Berry, Frankie Avalon, Jimmy Clanton, Jo-Ann Campbell, Jackie Wilson, Harvey and the Moonglows, Bo Diddley and
his Band, Eddie Cochran, the Flamingoes, "Baby" Washington,
the Crests, the Nu-Tornadoes, the Cadillacs, Dion and the Belmonts, Inga (who was Freed's wife), Ed Townsend, Gino and
Gina, and the Alan Freed Orchestra featuring Sam (the Man)
Taylor, King Curtis, George Auld and Earl Warren. Although
Ritchie's name was put in the program, his picture was not which
may have indicated a belated arrangement.

The featured film accompanying the "Jubilee" was *Villa* starring César Romero. There were about three to five shows a day
interspersed with the showing of the film and members of the

audience would often stay for two or three shows, paying one price. This author recalls that the Everly Brothers ended the first half of the show with a short intermission, while Bo Diddley ended the finale in which all the stars came on stage. When Ritchie appeared on stage, he wore a blue satin shirt with studded black vest and pants, which was very effective with stage lighting. He had obtained this outfit from Nudie's in North Hollywood, famous for their costumes for Hollywood celebrities and cowboy stars. The outfit was not as flashy as most clothes produced by this firm, yet it did reflect a similarity to the *charro* outfit often worn by Mexcian musicans and dancers.

Although the performances started in the morning and lasted until late at night, there was time for members of the show to get together or go out to view a few sights. There were also room parties because all the members stayed at the Plaza Hotel. Eddie Cochran used to give quite a few parties in his room. Ritchie and Eddie often appeared on the same bill in California, but it was at these room parties that they met for the first time and really got to know each other. "Ritchie was with us most of the time," said Sheeley. "Eddie adored him like a little brother and was a big fan of Ritchie's and vice versa." Other artists had room parties as well and Ritchie also hung around with members of the Crests and the Nu-Tornadoes. He had brought a movie camera and a still camera with him to New York and a film survives of him fooling around backstage with members of the Nu-Tornadoes, as well as photos he took.

At one of the room party gatherings, Ritchie met Diane Olsen, a pretty brunette who lived in New York. Little is known about her but she may have also been a singer and guitarist. She appears in the surviving film clip of Ritchie backstage, as well as in two photos taken with him. Their relationship remains debatable to the present, from Sheeley never recalling Ritchie with a girl during the Christmas show, to the Reyes definitely affirming a serious relationship, more so than with Donna Ludwig. According to one fanzine, Ritchie had wanted to give her an engagement ring which she refused until she could meet his family to obtain their approval. The Reyes did not recall this, but Mrs. Reyes attested that Ritchie was very close to Diane during his stay in New York, and very secretive about their relationship. Ritchie, as was true of many young rock idols of the day, did not want it to get out that he might have been going with a girl. Such information usually changed the image and popularity of a rock 'n' roll star. Photos were taken of the two together which were not released until after Ritchie's death.

Ritchie also met the featured stars of the show including Bo Diddley who took pictures of him according to the Reyes, Frankie Avalon, the Everly Brothers (a picture survives of Ritchie with them), and Chuck Berry. In addition, he made an appearance on "The Dick Clark Show" singing "Donna" which aired December 27th, and possibly one on "American Bandstand" and the Alan Freed TV show. Ritchie apparently did not get much chance to see many New York sights, although Duane Eddy, who was appearing in town, remembered going out with Ritchie and Eddie to search for a Mexican restaurant. He also recalled Ritchie "thumbing down" the one they found.

Ritchie and Keane also spent time with Carl Bloomberg of Allied Distributing. Bloomberg had four daughters who wanted Ritchie to sing at their school. This probably occurred shortly after New Year's, possibly on the Monday that Ritchie was to fly back to the Coast. Accordingly, he sang at their school in Hazel, New Jersey, just a few hours before leaving for Los Angeles.

Upon returning to L.A., Ritchie appeared in the Hal Wallis movie *Go Johnny Go* filmed at Hal Roach studios in Hollywood, famous in the past for Laurel and Hardy movies. New York D.J. Alan Freed, fondly known as "Mr. Rock 'n' Roll," for his coinage of that term, had promoted a series of rock 'n' roll films for those who were unable to attend his ongoing holiday shows in New York. *Go Johnny Go* was the last of these Freed-promoted rock movies. The black and white film starred not only Freed but also featured Jimmy Clanton, Sandy Stewart and Chuck Berry in speaking roles; Eddie Cochran, Ritchie Valens, the Flamingoes, Jackie Wilson, the Cadillacs, Harvey Fuqua (*sans* Moonglows), and Jo-Ann Campbell.

The movie was intended to be a bouncy, lighthearted experience, not unlike the old juke-box films of the 40's, this time with rock 'n' roll, and with the performances being more memorable than the actual story plot. Unfortunately, it was not made clear to the participants that the only benefit they would get from the movie was publicity. The only ones paid were those who had speaking roles. In the major scene where Ritchie appears, he is conversing with three girls at the table when Chuck Berry intervenes for him to play. Berry says, "We always have Ritchie

Valens to soothe your gentle nerves(?) . . ." Freed answers with "Swinging!" "Hey!" Berry calls to Ritchie—pan shot of Ritchie talking to the girls; he turns to Berry—"Let's sing for Mr. Freed. He might even play your record if it's rockin' enough." Here, Ritchie brings out a guitar and starts playing the song, "Ooh, My Head." Although this particular scene is *clearly* an acting scene regardless of whether he spoke or not, Ritchie was never paid for it.

As mentioned before, Ritchie did sing "Ooh, My Head," but there has been a rumor that he also sang "Dooby Dooby Wah" in the movie. There is no verification that Ritchie ever sang that particular song for the film, however, in the intro shots of the film, he wears a different outfit from the one worn in the "Little Queenie (sung by Chuck Berry)/Ooh, My Head" sequence. In another sequence, there is a poster and a marquee with Ritchie's name on it for a show that followed which featured Eddie Cochran and Jo-Ann Campbell and Harvey Fuqua. Ritchie may have sung another number for that show which was later edited from the sequence.

Ritchie wore a rather loud tweed suit in the promotional screen test photos for the film. In the "Little Queenie/Ooh, My Head" sequence, he wears a more toned-down darker tweed sportscoat with a round lapel, and a dark shirt with a mandarin collar with a white "wave" design across the chest. This outfit minimized his heavy appearance more so than the tweed suit. Ritchie played a light-colored Gibson guitar, which was probably a prop as it suspiciously resembles the guitar Cochran also played in the film. In the sequence, Ritchie sits with three girls in a place that seems to be a cross between a soda shop and a night club, clapping and snapping his fingers in a rather natural way while Berry plays and virtually dances with his guitar. Freed joins in this "jam session" with some obvious monotonous drumming. (Except for three numbers by Clanton and Stewart, all the songs in the film were pre-recorded on the performers' labels.) However comfortable or uneasy Ritchie may have felt in front of the movie camera, he continued to perform in a manner that was typical of him, adding a rather playful and teasing style with the girls, performing more for them than for Freed. It is one of the more memorable performances in the film.

The majority of *Go Johnny Go* was shot in Hollywood, with some sequences shot in New York. The film shows the marquee

of the Alan Freed Christmas "Jubilee" and is probably proof that
Go Johnny Go was indeed filmed after the 1958 show. The film
was released to theaters nationwide in August, 1959, with the
appendage "late" attached to Ritchie's name. However, it is possible that he saw the final screening of the film (with or without the
editing of "Dooby Dooby Wah"), because of a rather modest
statement he was supposed to have made regarding his role in
the film: "I'm not much good but I hope my mother likes me."

*   *   *

During the early part of January, more recordings and demos were done in Keane's home and at Gold Star. The Bo Diddley influence became more apparent in Ritchie's guitar playing.
These latter tapings filled out both *Ritchie* and the *Pacoima Junior
High School* albums. Appearances were in order more than ever,
and on Sunday, January 11th, Ritchie appeared, along with the
Collins Kids, Bobby Darin, Gary Crosby (son of Bing Crosby),
and Sam Butera and the Witnesses, in the first rock and roll
prime-time TV series outside of "The Dick Clark Show."

"The Music Shop," an NBC production, based in Hollywood,
was hosted by a well-respected music conductor and arranger,
Buddy Bregman, and was telecast on Sundays at 7:30 EST as a
half-hour variety show. "The Music Shop" was certainly the first
"rock and roll" program featured in color. "I remember," said
Keane, "going to the producer's house with Ritchie to watch the
show, because he had one of the first color television sets." This
was also the first time that Ritchie Valens was the featured guest,
even above the already famed Bobby Darin and Gary Crosby!
Ritchie's name appeared first in the headline advertisement in
the news, probably because he had the most recent hits with
"Donna/La Bamba." In addition, this was the first time that "La
Bamba" was sung, or rather lip-synched, as was also done on
"American Bandstand" and "The Dick Clark Show" on a major
TV show. However, the record was played and in one instance on
"American Bandstand," some Bandstand regulars got together
and made up a dance called "La Bamba," which went nowhere
because shortly afterward, Ritchie was killed. On "The Music
Shop," Ritchie sang "La Bamba" behind a screen with silhouet-
ting scenery, reminiscent of an Hispanic decor. Ritchie also sang
"Donna" on the show, again, to a recording, a curious paradox in

which Bregman presented all of his performers, even though there was a live band on the show! "The Music Shop" was probably Ritchie's last TV appearance and in less than two months after its January, 1959, debut, it was cancelled by NBC.

Sometime around January, Ritchie was signed to a long-term contract with General Artist Corporation (GAC), a booking agency responsible for rock and roll package tours. According to a *Variety* article, and to manager Keane, GAC was planning an "extensive buildup" for Ritchie. The first of these tours was to be the "Winter Dance Party" which would travel throughout the Midwest, primarily in the states of Minnesota, Wisconsin and Iowa. Following would be four weeks of theater engagements set for Baltimore, Washington, D.C., Philadelphia and New York. Outside of the GAC tour, there was also to be an appearance on "The Perry Como Show" and that summer, a possible trip to Europe and Australia. The Midwest tour was to be an exciting event for Ritchie simply in that this would be his first actual tour, travelling with other performers.

Ritchie had two more appearances to make before leaving on that fateful tour. One of them, "The Teen Canteen Show," sponsored by TV host "Jolly" Joe Yokum, was held on Saturday, January 17th at West Covina High School and was tabbed as a "Youth Rally" featuring two five-piece bands and other acts such as Lindsay Crosby (another son of Bing), the Vogues, the Accents, the Hollywood Flames, Dick D'Agostine and his Swingers, the Brown Brothers, the Four Dots and Sam Cooke, with Ritchie Valens headlining the show.

Another performance, which may have also been on the 17th (according to both Mrs. Reyes and Mrs. Beckett), was a show held at the Long Beach Civic Auditorium. Little is known about the show, who sponsored it, or who were the acts, with the exception of Dick Dale, who may have been one of the performers. Despite the distance between West Covina and Long Beach, both shows could have featured Ritchie; via freeways, Ritchie could have gone from one show to another in half an hour. Also, the headliner usually is the last to perform in a show. Mrs. Beckett distinctly remembered talking to Ritchie around 9 or 10 P.M. at Long Beach, and remembered his saying that he had to go to another engagement. She remembered that particular night being extremely foggy. The Reyes also attested to that fact because they drove Ritchie to the shows, and remembered his being quite anxious about the fog. At the Long Beach Civic, Mrs. Reyes recalled that while walking into the auditorium, she was aware that people were already recognizing Ritchie. When he asked her to hold his jacket, one twelve-year-old girl ran up to her to try to grab it away, begging her to let her have it. "But the jacket belongs to Ritchie Valens!" the young girl protested. In the light of these two concerts, Ritchie had joined the ranks as a bona-fide teen idol.

Gail Smith had some special recollections about the last day before Ritchie went on the tour: "Connie [Ritchie's mother], Ritchie, my mother and I went to church the night before Ritchie was going to leave on tour. It was at Guardian Angels on Laurel Canyon Blvd. Ritchie and I knelt down and prayed together for a safe trip. On the way home, while our mothers sat up front, we were sitting in the back seat talking about the upcoming tour. Ritchie was really anxious to meet the Big Bopper. He thought it was funny when the Bopper said, 'Helooo baaby!' Also, Ritchie said, 'When I get back, I'm gonna get my T-Bird.' I said, 'You're kidding!' That was the biggest deal in the world, because I couldn't imagine anyone having that much money. He wanted to take me with him to pick out the color and I remember saying that I wanted it blue, because that was the color he wanted. I also asked him at the time if he was afraid of airplanes. And he said, 'Well, I'm getting used to it, but I am [still] afraid of them.' I added, 'It's snowing back there and there are storms. What'd you do if you crash?' And he said, 'I'll land on my guitar!' It was quite a discussion that set my priorities on how I felt about Ritchie and carrying on his future and memory."

Around the 19th or 20th of January, Ritchie had a farewell party at his home, before leaving for New York and Chicago, to begin the Midwest "Winter Dance Party" tour. Ritchie's party also served as a kind of housewarming, since he had just purchased a new stucco house located on Remington Street in Pacoima with a $1,000 down payment, nearly a month earlier. Members of the Silhouettes as well as other friends and relatives attended the party. Donna Fox recalled that Ritchie called her that night and asked her to come. "My father wouldn't let me go and I cried," she said. "Ritchie called me up twice that night and said he would miss me and see me as soon as he got back." The party lasted all night and into the morning. Because of his apparent fear of flying, Ritchie was known to stay up all night, especially when he had to catch a plane, so that he could sleep on it. The Reyes drove him to the airport, but this time, Ritchie's older brother, Bob, also came. Bob Morales lived separately with his own family and the two seldom got a chance to get together. That last time, Ritchie walked up to his brother, put his arms around him and said, "I want you to take care of my mother . . ."

The Winter Dance Party

The "Winter Dance Party" was an example of touring shows that helped promote rock and roll and GAC had held previous tours with a multitude of acts. But there were marked differences with this particular tour. It was the worst time of the year to have such a tour, especially in the Midwest where the winters are most severe. Yet, there was a guarantee of good reception despite the weather, for such shows which featured acts performing their hits with *live* accompaniment drew crowds in these areas far out of proportion to the size of the local populations. Another difference was that former GAC tours had featured as many as twenty acts. This time, there were only five: Ritchie Valens, Frankie Sardo, J.P. Richardson (called the "Big Bopper"), Buddy Holly and the Crickets (not the original members, but Tommy Allsup, Charlie "Goose" Bunch and Waylon Jennings), and Dion and the Belmonts. Of the five, Buddy Holly was a veteran rocker with several hits to boot, including "Peggy Sue," "Maybe Baby" and "That'll Be the Day." The Big Bopper had recently scored a hit with the song "Chantilly Lace," and Dion and the Belmonts had hits with "I Wonder Why," "Don't Pity Me," and "No One Knows." Only Frankie Sardo did not have any top forty hits. A potential hopeful, Sardo would open the "Winter Dance Party" by singing some of the current popular songs which were not his own. Allsup, Bunch and Jennings as the Crickets backed up all of the performers. Ritchie probably sang "Donna" and "La Bamba," but it is not really known whether he also sang "Come On, Let's Go," "Boney-Maronie" or the soon to be released "That's My Little Suzie." However, most of the acts did at least three or four songs to help fill out a show that lasted three to four hours.

Irwin Feld was the ongoing promoter for GAC rock shows. Rod Lucier was the road manager of the "Winter Dance Party" and the only one travelling who was not a performer. The tour probably took off from Chicago about the 21st or 22nd of January. On the 23rd, they were to begin their first show at George Devine's Ballroom in Milwaukee, Wisconsin. Outside, it was 25° below zero and the artists wondered whether there would be a show until they saw lines of teenagers standing outside virtually for blocks. Fortunately, the artists stayed in a hotel that night, a luxury they were denied within the next few days. Leaving Milwaukee, it was quickly discovered that their bus contained a heater that could not keep out the Wisconsin winter. Keeping warm on the bus became the main concern of the occupants and they would have to huddle together, wrapped in all the clothing they could find, occasionally drinking alcohol to help reverse the chill a little bit. Before the "Winter Dance Party" tour was over, they would have been in seven or eight buses, all with very poor heaters.

The artists moved on to Kenosha, Wisconsin on January 24th (pictures survive of the concert); played on the 25th at the Kato Ballroom in Kanato, Wisconsin; the 26th at Eau Claire, Wisconsin (pictures survive); the 27th at the Fiesta Ballroom, Montevideo, Minnesota (pictures survive); the Prom Ballroom at St. Paul, Minnesota on the 28th; the 29th at the Capital Theater in Davenport, Iowa; the 30th at the Lamarr Ballroom in Fort Dodge, Iowa (a picture of Ritchie survives in color from this concert); and on the 31st at the Armory in Duluth, Minnesota.

Upon leaving Duluth, the bus froze up and the troupe had to huddle in coats and newspapers to keep warm. A truck and a sheriff had to take the members to a nearby town and Charlie Bunch, the drummer for the troupe, suffered frostbite and had to remain in the hospital for several days. The artists had to play at the Cinderella Ballroom in Appleton, Wisconsin, on the afternoon of the 1st of February, then take a train to Green Bay for the evening show at the Riverside Ballroom. The drumming was to be divided for the rest of the tour among Buddy, Ritchie and one of the members of the Belmonts. It is known that Ritchie played drums for the Belmonts' songs. A picture survives in color of this event. Another picture in color of Ritchie backstage shows a very tired and extremely sober young man, looking far older than seventeen years. As the photographer Larry Matti later recalled: "We remember Ritchie Valens as being very quiet and staying out of most of the good-natured banter that took place backstage. But that all seemed to disappear when he went onstage in his blue satin shirt and black studded vest and pants. It was like he lived for those moments onstage and made the most of them when they came. He also seemed to really enjoy the added opportunity of playing the drums that night." Besides the familiar black outfit with the blue satin shirt, Ritchie would also appear on stage in a vertical-striped sequined shirt with a black sweater, or a dark sweater (possibly navy blue) with a white V-neck collar and a white stripe on the front (which he also wore at the Pacoima Junior High School assembly), or a red shirt with horizontal designs, usually worn with the dark blue or the black sweater. He also had a dark overcoat which he borrowed from his manager and was expecting another coat from his mother which he asked her to send, and a pair of light pants which he wore on the fatal flight.

After the successful Green Bay show, the troupe headed out to Clear Lake, Iowa, in a converted school bus. Again, it had engine trouble and the school bus did not pull into Clear Lake until 6:00 P.M., two hours before a show that would last four hours! It had been six days since the troupe had stayed at a hotel and their stage clothes were getting rumpled and soiled. The clothes of the Crickets literally had road dirt on them. In Clear Lake, Buddy had decided to charter a plane that he, Waylon and Tommy would fly ahead in, some four hundred miles to Fargo, North Dakota, the closest airport to Moorehead, Minnesota. Buddy felt that his tiredness would affect his stage appearance and by going ahead of the troupe, the sorely needed laundering would be done. Lucier, the road manager, encouraged the flight because Buddy and the others would also take care of any business problems that might arise. They all agreed to share the one hundred eight dollar cost of the flight. The others would travel four hundred thirty miles on the bus to Moorehead, Minnesota, hopefully to get a few hours rest in a hotel. That night in Clear Lake, at the Surf Ballroom, Buddy asked the manager of the Ballroom, Carroll Anderson, to charter a plane. Anderson called Dwyer's Flying Service, a local charter air service. The owner of the air charter, Jerry Dwyer, was unavailable but a young assistant, Roger Peterson, agreed to the flight, even though it was his day off.

The story has been told before of how Ritchie approached Tommy Allsup to give up his seat on the plane. Allsup was also large-framed and did not like the idea of giving up his seat and he initially refused. But Ritchie persisted, saying, "I have never been on a small plane before. Please let me go instead." As the bus was being loaded after the show and Tommy returned from the bus to check his gear, Ritchie again approached him and repeated his request. "Come on, let's flip a coin," said Ritchie. "Heads I go, tails you go." " I get Bopper's sleeping bag if I lose," said Allsup. "It would also be okay if Buddy had no objections." The coin was flipped and it came up heads.

But the story has *not* been told of *why* Ritchie wanted to take a small plane, especially if he had a fear of them. It can only be speculated as to the "why." The Bopper approached Waylon Jennings for his seat as it was uncomfortable for him to ride on the bus because of his large frame. He was also suffering from a severe cold. Jennings later related that *both* the Bopper and Ritchie had colds. A confirmation has never been made as to whether Ritchie was coming down with a cold, but even if he was, he may not have said that much to any of the others. Being the youngest and possibly feeling that the others might think he could not "take" the tour, he could have kept silent about the matter. It is known that Ritchie called his manager from either Duluth or Green Bay and told him how miserable things were. "I talked with him from 'Jacks on the Pier' in Santa Monica," said Keane. "I told him to finish that evening and then come home if things were that bad." Also during that call, Keane told Ritchie that "Donna" would shortly go "gold" and that when he returned he would receive it. Ritchie also told Keane that he received two curtain calls in the Duluth performance. For him to "skip out" on the beleaguered "Winter Dance Party" tour seemed highly unlikely. It was simply not his style, but probably like other members of the troupe, Ritchie may have been concerned about the effect the trip was having on his stage performance and felt that being the performer with the top ten hit, this concern should be dealt with, despite any personal feelings he may have had about flying in small planes. This conclusion, though speculative, is fairly reasonable about one who would find time between professional engagements just to sing for a school assembly, as he had done for San Fernando, Pacoima and the school in New Jersey. Buddy did not object to Ritchie's accompanying him. Apparently, they had become friends on the tour. "It was the first time they met," Buddy's mother related in a letter. "Buddy didn't know if he was going to like Ritchie at first (he probably thought that Ritchie, being a teenager, would be a little rambunctious as Paul Anka initially was), but he found him to be a great guy." Mrs. Holley also related that Buddy was planning for Ritchie to visit him that summer.

Between 1,100 and 1,500 young people showed up for the Clear Lake performance, some coming from as far as Illinois and Minnesota. Bob Hale was a local D.J. and the master of ceremonies. The show began as usual with Frankie Sardo, then Ritchie Valens, the Big Bopper, Dion and the Belmonts and Buddy Holly. Both Buddy and a member of the Belmonts, Carlo Mastrangelo, played drums that night. Hale remembered that each act played two sets and even recalled fifteen minutes of "goofing off," in which Buddy, Ritchie and the Bopper attempted singing as a trio.

Around midnight, Anderson drove the three entertainers to the Mason City Airport and it was about 12:40 A.M. that they were met by both Peterson and Dwyer. According to Peterson, weather conditions were adequate for the flight, even though the winds were blowing and light snow was falling. According to Anderson, the sky was clear and the stars could be seen in the 18° cold. However, the airport did not inform Peterson of several advisories which had just come in from the U.S. Weather Bureau. The warnings necessitated instrument flying and Peterson had previously failed his test on instrument flight check because he could not keep a proper altitude. Anderson helped the three performers load their baggage on the red four-seater Beechcraft Bonanza. Ritchie and the Bopper climbed into the back seats while Buddy climbed in front alongside Peterson. Around 1:00 A.M., the single engine plane took off. Anderson returned home and Dwyer went to the control tower. When the plane was about four miles out from the airport, Dwyer thought he saw the plane descend, then vanish, but dismissed it as an "optical illusion." However, when the pilot failed to immediately report a flight plan back to Dwyer, he became worried and checked in with other nearby airports. Shortly before dawn, an alert was issued for the missing aircraft and Dwyer personally flew to retrace Peterson's course. He spotted the wreckage eight miles northwest of the Mason City airfield. It was approximately 9:35 A.M.

Police arrived at the crash site shortly thereafter. The wreckage and the bodies lay in a cornfield several hundred yards from a farmhouse belonging to an Albert Juhl. The body of J.P. Rich-ardson was thrown forty feet from the wreckage while those of Holly and Valens were thrown twenty feet. Peterson's body was still in the wreckage. Anderson was called from Clear Lake to make the identification. Because a black wallet was found near the plane belonging to Tommy Allsup, there was some confusion as to the identities. Tommy had given the wallet to Buddy so that a registered letter could be picked up. The rest of the troupe did not arrive in Moorehead until 12:30 that afternoon. Waylon, Tommy and Lucier went in to register the rest of the troupe at the hotel when Tommy noticed the Bopper's picture on the TV screen. The set was very low. After talking with the desk clerk who notified them of the accident, Tommy brought the news to the rest on the bus. Almost immediately, everyone called home. In both Tommy's and Waylon's cases, their families thought they were dead.

The mandatory notification of the next of kin before media announcements are made did not apply until the early 60's. The initial radio announcements were confused in Texas where Bud-dy, Tommy, Waylon and the Bopper originated. There may have been some initial confusion as well when the announcement reached California. Donna Fox recalled, "My girlfriend heard it on her little portable radio and when she told me, I just couldn't believe it. I was in shock. I called Ritchie's mother right away and as soon as she answered I knew she was crying. But she said they had hopes that it wasn't him. I made it through school—they wouldn't let me go home. After school, I went right over to Mrs. Valenzuela's house. The newsmen were all over the place and I could've hit them all right in the mouth. We finally got in with all those assholes around and when I got to her she was just in shock. She could do nothing but rock back and forth. I remem-ber her holding me. She let me go into Ritchie's room and see his things. She told me if I wanted it, I could have his gold record of 'Donna' but I told her no, she needed that for herself. She told me I could have one of his guitars, but I told her these were hers, for her children; hopefully little Mario when he grew up would take Ritchie's place."

Other relatives and close friends were able to make their way into the newly purchased stucco home. A table was set up with Ritchie's picture; some flowers and his two guitars, a Gibson and the little turquoise green guitar Ritchie first played upon, were placed before it.

Because Ritchie was the youngest and the teenager of the three with the current hit, most fan magazines saw the opportunity to eulogize him and record this incident, regardless of the veracity of Ritchie's life story; because Hollywood was nearby, the story for these magazines was close enough to home for them to publicize. A couple of magazines had actually approached Ritchie before the tragedy; now the majority of them saw a ripe story to sell. Ritchie Valens was the first rock and roll performer who was immediately exploited within *hours* of his death.

The "Winter Dance Party" tour continued in Moorehead, Minnesota, even though many of the members were very reluctant. That night, February 3rd, Frankie Sardo opened with a few words and sang Ritchie's "Donna." Moist eyes from the audience greeted the tune. The tour that was to bring happiness and fun to the Midwest became from that day on, somewhat of a memorial service for the three fallen stars. A local band and a local singer Bob Velline (who later became famous as "Bobby Vee") did most of Holly's tunes that night. GAC made financial and miscellaneous promises to the troupe members if they would continue the winter tour. None of the verbal promises made, especially those to Allsup and Jennings, were kept, including flying down to Holly's funeral. A spokesman for Irwin Feld later told *Billboard* that the tour would continue to its conclusion, saying, "We always fought against the idea of any of them chartering their own planes." The spokesman did not mention how poorly the buses were heated or the engine trouble. On February 4th, the tour continued to Sioux City, Iowa where teen idols Frankie Avalon and Jimmy Clanton substituted for the deceased stars. The tour then went on to the cities of Des Moines and Cedar Rapids, Iowa; Spring Valley and Chicago, Illinois; Waterloo and Dubuque, Iowa; Louisville, Kentucky; Canton and Youngstown, Ohio; finishing up February 14th and 15th at Peoria and Springfield, Illinois.

*   *   *

For the next three days, people poured into the house on Remington Street, mostly kids from nearby junior high and high schools throughout the San Fernando Valley and other L.A.

communities coming to pay their respects to Ritchie's family. Diane Olsen personally flew out from New York to be with his mother. Said Smith, "Diane was very much in grief and related to me several stories and things that Ritchie said. It sounded as if he was very much crazy about her. They had spent a lot of time together before he left for the winter tour." The Hispanic Catholic tradition of saying the rosary in Spanish at the home of the deceased had to be postponed for nearly a month after the crash because Mrs. Valenzuela was too ill to participate. Eventually, the phone number had to be changed for, it must be said, unfortunately, there were harrassing phone calls expressing gladness that Ritchie was dead! The family has related that there was much jealousy towards Ritchie's success. Others in the Valley, especially talented musicians and singers, either from Pacoima Junior High or San Fernando High felt it unfair that Ritchie had become famous virtually overnight. Some of these more aggressive local performers felt "cheated" that this shy, stocky youngster should suddenly come into fame and "fortune." There also may have been some regard for Ritchie's ancestry, but it seemed apparent that some of the harrassment also came, sad to say, from members within the Hispanic community.

Ritchie's body was shipped back by train to the West Coast. Identifications were made by both Morales and Keane. Then his body was taken to Noble Chapel Funeral Home in San Fernando. The wake was held on Friday, February 6th and the funeral, on Saturday morning, the 7th. It took place at St. Ferdinand's Catholic Church in San Fernando, the church that Ritchie was probably baptized in as a child. People came from all over the West to attend. "The thing that made me the maddest at the funeral were the photographers," said Donna Fox. "They were like a bunch of bloodhounds. I remember one photographer trying to take my picture and I knocked the camera out of his hand."

Over 1,000 people attended the services at which the Rev. William Lynch gave the sermon. Sharon Sheeley, Cochran's fiancée, remembered how horribly upset Cochran was about Ritchie, but since he was closer to Buddy's family, he decided to attend Buddy's funeral, while she attended Ritchie's. Members of the Silhouettes including Walter Préndez, Armando Ortiz, Walter Takaki and possibly the Jones brothers, were the pall bearers.

The day was remembered as damp, if not raining, yet crowds of people accompanied family and friends to the San Fernando Mission cemetery where Ritchie was buried. Said Rocha, "After the funeral, I came home and cried like a baby for a very long time."

9

WHATEVER HAPPENED TO
THE LEGEND OF RITCHIE VALENS?

The Tributes

Aside from the newspaper reports around the country, the deaths of Ritchie Valens, J.P. Richardson and Buddy Holly went unnoticed by the adult media. A good example is the *New York Times,* one of the most highly respected and liberal newspapers in the country. It was also known at the time to be biased in its view of rock 'n' roll and there was no mention of the fatal plane crash. The reaction of the booking agency and the trades was not any better with a definite "business as usual" attitude. Only Mercury Records bought a full-page ad in *Bilboard* to honor the Bopper. As 1959 progressed, bits and pieces of articles related to the three performers began to appear in both *Billboard* and *Variety.*

Within hours of Valens', Richardson's and Holly's deaths, a disc jockey from San Bernardino, California, Tommy Dee, decided to write a song commemorating the tragedy he had announced earlier. The following day, he brought the song, appropriately titled, "Three Stars," to American Music Publishers. Originally, he had intended for Eddie Cochran to record the song, which Cochran did. Eddie was also scheduled to be on the "Winter Dance Party" and for him this was a personal tragedy since both Valens and Holly had been close friends. His intention was to donate the money from the song to the families of the three victims. But problems arose with his recording company. A single of Cochran's "Three Stars" was never released. Fourteen months after the three stars' deaths, Cochran also perished in an automobile accident in England.

As a precaution, Tommy Dee personally recorded the song on the Crest label (Crest 1057) with Carol Kay and the Teenairs backing his spoken eulogy. Dee's recording, despite competition from a cover by Ruby Wright (on King 5192), reached No. 11 on the *Billboard* Top 100.

"Three Stars," which describes the characteristics of each singer as Dee recalled them, has been accepted as "corny" or, at best, "maudlin sentimentality." Yet, this song is a continuation of a tradition which is far more in the mode of a "folk song" than a "rock ballad." The practice of composing a song shortly on the heels of a tragedy, called a "broadside ballad," can be traced far back into the tradition of English literature. The religious sentiments expressed in the song coincide with the Americana of folk, gospel and country music. The emotional honesty of Eddie Cochran's version of the song more nearly expresses the message the song was meant to convey.

Several other songs were recorded to commemorate the tragic event: "The Great Tragedy" by Hershel Almond (Ace 558), "Gold Records in the Snow" by Benny Barnes (D 1052), and "Three Young Men" by Lee Davis (Cub 9026), all in the country-western/hillbilly tradition. Other songs included "Three Friends" by Scott Wood (Beat 1008), and "Gone Too Soon" by Chuck Travis (Energy 105). Special mention should be made of two songs: "Buddy, Big Bopper and Ritchie" by Loretta Thompson (Skoop 1050), meant as a tribute by those who saw them perform on the "Winter Dance Party" tour, and "The Ballad of Donna and Peggy Sue," by Ray Campi (D 1047) in which the singer imitates the melodies of the hits by Valens and Holly. Other songs which specifically mention Ritchie Valens include Waylon Jennings' "The Stage" (Trend 106), in which he refers to Ritchie as the "La Bamba King," and Johnny Cymbal's "Teenage Heaven" (Kapp 6853), in which he "sees" Ritchie singing "Donna."

There were three tribute songs that particularly had to do with Ritchie and his hit "Donna": "Lost Without You"/"Now That You're Gone" by Donna (Ludwig/Fox) (Pop 1103), and "A Letter to Donna" by the Kittens (Unart 29081). Donna Fox recalled with some embarrassment, "It seemed like after Ritchie died, all of a sudden, my father thought, 'Gee, what a nice guy he was.' I was very disgusted with that. But I was young and did what he told me to do. My silly father went and got me an agent.

That was what was so funny! I was so untalented. I seemed to have been hoodwinked into that song. I can't sing and I'll be the first one to tell you! I made the record under pressure from my father and from Huggy Boy, a D.J. from Los Angeles, who owned Pop Records. He told me that if I didn't want the money from the recording, if it made any money, that I could give it to Mrs. Valenzuela. So I signed a contract with him, stating that any proceeds from that record would go to Mrs. Valenzuela. Now, to this day, I don't know if she received a cent. I did appear on some television shows — "Art Laboe" was one program I appeared on — and I never received any money for that. The recording wasn't much of a success, so I assume if Mrs. Valenzuela received any money, it wasn't very much."

The songs "Now That You're Gone" b/w "Lost Without You" attempted to carry over and create the legend of Ritchie and Donna's relationship, initially exploited by teen fanzines. One extreme example of this exploitation culminated with a sensationalist newspaper article in Germany which stated that Ritchie and Donna were married! Furthermore, it stated that a whole cult evolved around the song "Donna," in which teens dressed in black and mourned while playing the song (!) At most, Donna's recordings, not so much for the singing as for the words, should be viewed as a time-piece of 50's teen maudlin sentimentality. The same can also be said about a lesser known recording by the Kittens, "A Letter to Donna." The idea of this song seemed more "appropriate;" in it the Kittens "comfort" Donna in her "mourning" over Ritchie's death. The "letter" concept coincided with the many letters Donna received from all over the country and the world expressing their feelings for Ritchie and her. Said Donna, "I received close to a thousand fan letters from people throughout the U.S. I received letters from all over the world — Thailand, Germany, China, Hong Kong, many from Canada and Mexico. I'm sure I answered every single one of them. I even received a letter from a fellow in prison who wanted me to write to him about Ritchie. It was quite touching to me to think that people cared that much."

Valens fans not only wrote to Donna and to Ritchie's family, they also wrote to Del-Fi requesting more of Ritchie's songs. Initially, Del-Fi had special plans of its own. Besides releasing the long-awaited first LP, *Ritchie Valens*, during the month of February, 1959, by April, Keane presented radio station KFWB with a gold record of "Donna." He also presented one to Mrs. Valen-zuela the following month, possibly at an American Legion Hall Memorial Dance, and in June of that year, he announced plans to establish a memorial fund supported by the sale of all future Valens releases.

A special series with a gold label plus a souvenir four-color jacket showing an autographed photo of Ritchie, known as the "Limited Valens Memorial Series," was released as the 45-single, "We Belong Together," backed by the previously unreleased "Little Girl" (DF 4117). This first of the series was to be backed with "heavy national advertising and promotion." Included also in the first release were announcements on special unpublished photos of Ritchie and a Valens memorial booklet to satisfy the thousands of requests by fans. The fund, with its special releases, would contribute to a Young People's Center in Pacoima. This memorial center never came about, probably because of legal and financial disputes between Del-Fi and the Valens estate. As for the "Limited Valens Memorial Series," one other 45-single was released around 1960, "Stay Beside Me," backed by "Big Baby Blues" (DF 4128), the latter having been released earlier under "Arvee Allens."

"That's My Little Suzie"/"In A Turkish Town" was the first posthumous release (March, 1959). The last single release of a Ritchie Valens song was "Cry, Cry, Cry," b/w "Paddiwack Song" in 1960; the last LP with "new" material was the *Pacoima Junior High School Concert Album,* released in December of that year. There were no more Valens releases until April, 1963, almost two and a half years later! These were *Ritchie Valens Greatest Hits Memorial Album* (DF 1225), followed by *His Greatest Hits, Vol. 2* (DF 1247). The gap may have occurred for a number of reasons. For one thing, Keane decided to divert more attention to pro-moting other artists including Chan Romero, who was to be Ritchie's "protégé," and the Carlos Brothers, as well as Johnny Crawford, then TV star of the "Rifleman" series. There may have also been financial problems unresolved with the Valens estate. Ironically, during the early 60's, there was an ongoing increasing interest in Valens' music overseas. Nonetheless, after 1963, little was done to preserve that interest.

Tributes to the Valens legacy also came in the form of dances around the southern California area. In 1959, there was a grand one at the El Monte Legion Stadium of which little is known or remembered, as well as one at the Long Beach Civic, at which Donna appeared. These may have occurred before May 13, 1959. On that date, which would have been Ritchie's eighteenth birthday, there was a special memorial service commemorating his birthday at the San Fernando Mission cemetery. Ritchie's mother got together several of his acquaintances and friends, mostly girls, including Donna, Lillian Rocha (Beckett), and Gail Smith, who was still president of the Valens Memorial Fan Club. Most of the girls were dressed in white party dresses. Mrs. Valenzuela was dressed mostly in black. A flower arrangement in the form of an electric guitar was placed by the gravesite. Pictures survive of this service but no more can be remembered of it. Curiously, Diane Olsen is absent from the photo. It may be because she suddenly and mysteriously left the confines of the Valenzuela household sometime between March and June, after she had stated to teen magazine reporters that she planned to stay with the family indefinitely. "I don't want to say anything against Diane," recalled Donna Fox. "I don't know her but I had a strong feeling that perhaps she came out here for a wee bit of publicity and was a little disappointed." There was a Memorial Dance that followed at the Legion Hall in San Fernando whereby Keane presented the gold record of "Donna" to Ritchie's mother. Since May 13, 1959, was a Wednesday night, the Memorial Dance could have been on the following Saturday, May 16th, although there is no recollection of the actual date.

In 1960, members of the Ritchie Valens Memorial fan clubs throughout the nation and overseas, in collaboration with Del-Fi and Bob Keane, proclaimed the month of February as "Ritchie Valens Month." The activities included among the clubs were parties and record hops. There was a special "Ritchie Valens Memorial Dance" at the El Monte Legion Stadium on February 20th, with KRLA's D.J.'s Frosty Harris and Jimmy O'Neill as MC's. Who appeared as guests on that show is not known. Another Valens Memorial Dance took place on February 25, 1961, at which Gil Rocha, a former Silhouette, played with the L.A. Imperials. This was the third Memorial Dance, held at El Monte Legion Stadium and hosted by Art Laboe. The last known Ritchie Valens Memorial Dance held in the Southern California area promoted on a "large" scale took place at the Long Beach Civic Auditorium on New Year's Eve, 1961. This particular dance holds special interest because it marks the first appearance of a group that later became known as the Beach Boys. The Beach Boys celebrated the twentieth anniversary of this appearance recently in 1981, at Long Beach on the Queen Mary. Over 20,000 fans showed up for the event, yet few knew that the Beach Boys got their start performing at a Ritchie Valens Memorial Dance.

There are three essential reasons why major activities surrounding the memory of Ritchie Valens declined so early. First, the "tribute shows," which were mostly confined to the L.A. area, gradually veered from their initial intention until the dances had to do with Ritchie Valens in name only. Close family and friends avoided certain "tribute shows," especially at El Monte Legion, because they often attracted the "wrong crowd" which at times resulted in physical conflicts. Also, D.J.'s sponsoring these events received most of the proceeds, while Ritchie's family received little or no remuneration, which prompted strong objection from the Valens estate. By 1962, there were no more "tribute shows" in the L.A. area.

Secondly, Ritchie's death left a painful void, not only among family and friends, but within the communities of Pacoima and San Fernando as well. Several policemen had been assigned to the funeral for fear that there might be a youthful demonstration which never came about. Ritchie was a success story from the neighborhood, the first Chicano in the late 50's to "make it." The tragedy fueled feelings of bitterness and distrust between family and friends and among friends. Relationships in which Ritchie had been the focal point began to slowly drift apart. Not knowing who to really blame for the accident, many in the community saw Bob Keane in the position of the "scapegoat." One incident Gil Rocha recalled after seeing *Go Johnny Go* at a drive-in: "After Ritchie came on, we sat there and honked our horns for five minutes. All of a sudden, the whole drive-in just started honking. That drive-in was packed for the whole week. We saw it about four or five times. Then we had the same feeling: 'He's dead! Why? Damn that Bob Keane!'"

Finally, the national/international president of the Ritchie Valens Memorial Club had business connections with Del-Fi and was also heading the Johnny Crawford Fan Club in 1962-64. Gail Smith, who later worked for Del-Fi, explains, "My personal feeling was that the Memorial Club was a business headed by Muriel Williams (the president). She would send out the information

Bob Keane wanted and I found her very difficult to deal with myself. Many times she felt I was too free with what I was doing. They [Williams and Del-Fi] wanted to keep everything black and white.

"From my experiences of working in the recording business, I became very cynical about music to the point where I don't like to hear music that much. Music is a business and it uses people." Long before Del-Fi's quiet demise in the summer of 1964, several of the chapters within this country were headed mostly by girls in their teens who eventually married and devoted their time to their families or diverted their interests to other male rock artists of the day. For most of them, the attraction to Ritchie was more "physical" than "musical," though that is not to say that it could not have been both. Ardent male fans of Ritchie's were mostly young Hispanic musicians who wanted to be like him. It was at a time when "fan clubs" as such were seen as something more "feminine." Furthermore, the music industry itself was leaning toward a more palatable and "acceptable" brand of rock music, trending toward a pop vein rather than a "down to the ground" rock and roll. It started with the likes of Frankie Avalon and Fabian, then onto idols like Bobby Vee (who ironically made his debut at the "Winter Dance Party" in Moorehead, Minnesota) and Bobby Vinton. (Best expressed of this musical change is Bobby Darin's early 1959 hit "Mack the Knife," a purely pop treatment from a former rock 'n' roller, which reached No. 1 for several weeks.) After 1964, with the demise of Del-Fi, fractions of the Memorial Club (actually, newly formed clubs) continued to survive in Europe, especially Germany and France. They lasted until 1966-67.

In 1960, in his attempt to seek out other talent, Keane formed a subsidiary of Del-Fi and named it after Ritchie's biggest hit, "Donna." Donna Records' first success was a singer from Seattle, Washington, by the name of Ron Holden who had a hit with "Love You So." Chan Romero and the Carlos Brothers on Del-Fi made waves locally, but it was not until mid-1961 that Del-Fi had another nationwide hit with "Those Oldies But Goodies" by Little Caesar and the Romans, the first Del-Fi recording to earn a gold record since Valens' "Donna." This was followed in 1962 with Johnny Crawford's hits, "Cindy's Birthday" and "Your Nose is Gonna Grow." Del-Fi continued to record Crawford and other artists with little success. Rene Hall offered another reason for Del-Fi's demise: "Keane was satisfying his own ambitions by wanting to record jazz, playing the clarinet. He was a fairly good clarinetist, but no Artie Shaw or Benny Goodman. He blew a lot of money making albums featuring himself playing that instrument. They were recorded at a time when that particular type of jazz wasn't selling. In my opinion, that was the *main* reason for the demise of Del-Fi."

In 1965, Keane re-formed a company with Mustang Records and became manager of the Bobby Fuller Four who had a smash hit with "I Fought the Law," a song ironically written by a friend of Buddy Holly's and a member of the post-Holly Crickets, Sonny Curtis. Fuller also met an untimely death, yet Keane continued to record other artists and takes pride in having made some of the first recordings for such late 60's and early 70's personalities as the Fifth Dimension, the Watts 103rd St. Rhythm Band, Frank Zappa and Barry White.

In the mid-60's, following the closure of Del-Fi, some Valens recordings began to appear on strange, low-budget labels. In the U.S., they were often poorly recorded. For example, *Ritchie Valens and Jerry Cole* on Crown Label (CST 336) (who, by the way, do *not* sing together), is considered by many record collectors as one of the poorest recorded LP's ever! Overseas, the sound quality was better, probably due to special European masters previously obtained from Del-Fi.

Keane soundly denies relegating any of the original masters from the Del-Fi vault, yet there strangely appears in the U.S. Guest Star recording an alternate take of "That's My Little Suzie," misnamed "Rock Little Donna." Guest Star and Crown may have been early forms of bootlegs recorded from records or accessible tapes, or they may have been budget versions of direct Del-Fi tapes. As early as 1960, the single "Donna/La Bamba" had reappeared on so many "oldies" labels and "Memory Lane" albums that it has been difficult to keep track of them.

Outside of the European LP releases, one more curious budget LP simply titled *Ritchie Valens* appeared in the early 70's as part of a series of other rock and pop artists on the MGM Label. The sound quality on the album seemed more "improved" than either Guest Star or Crown, but it is not known whether this album was strictly a bootleg. In 1981, Rhino Records in Los Angeles obtained the original masters and/or best recordings of Del-Fi material from Keane to put in a three-box record set with actual reproductions of the original covers of the three Del-Fi Valens LP's, and titled it *The History of Ritchie Valens*, with an additional single LP record, *The Best of Ritchie Valens* containing fourteen selections. These were the first releases of Valens material in the U.S. in nearly ten years.

The question of the royalties resulting over the years from the Del-Fi issues and releases is a topic as delicate as walking on eggshells. The royalties battle began while Ritchie was alive. Up to now, little has been said about Ritchie's relationship with Bob Keane. Keane contends that he treated Ritchie "like a son," and Ritchie always seemed to realize that Bob was responsible for discovering him. Sessions drummer Palmer said, "Their relationship in the studio always seemed amiable and cordial, never overly affectionate. I never heard them exchange words whatsoever."

However, according to the Reyes, they distinctly remembered Ritchie having considerable trouble with Keane. At the point when his career was well under way, he was seriously considering finding a new manager, the key area of dispute being money. Ritchie was frustrated that his own success was not yet allowing him to alleviate the financial struggle of his family. It was after an argument in which Ritchie lost his temper (supposedly at a recording session, though neither Stan Ross nor any of the sessions musicians recalled it) that Ritchie threatened to leave and Keane ended up giving him the $1,000 to put a down payment on a house for his mother. Since Ritchie was a minor, Ernestine and Lelo had to sign for the payment. Keane contends that this payment was a loan which was never paid back. Also, said Keane, "I alone made the arrangements for the funeral which cost me about $7,000." Yet, initially, there was no money to even place a gravestone where Ritchie was buried and the money had to be raised at one of the earlier memorial dances.

Mrs. Valenzuela had to take on a job to continue supporting the family until the settlement of the Valens estate was reached (toward the end of 1960) in which she received about $40,000. Prior to that time, she had also approached Ted Quillin asking for his assistance in expediting some of Ritchie's posthumous earnings. Quillin suggested that he may have been responsible for Ritchie's considering a new manager since he advised Ritchie to find someone who could take care of the portion of money he earned. Quillin remembered the late Ernie Freeman (who played piano on "La Bamba") telling him: "The problem with young recording stars is that they get rich before making any money." The former KFWB D.J. felt close enough to Ritchie to want to keep this from happening to him.

Several personnel in the music industry who worked with Keane have complained that they were not paid for their services in association with Del-Fi Records and/or its subsidiary. Said Ross of Gold Star: "[Keane] wasn't a great payer. I say this publicly because he still owed a lot of money even after a song was a hit. He owed me money for the sessions. You could work with him but you were always cautious about getting your money from him." Sharon Sheeley proclaimed that she was not paid for royalties from "Hurry Up." Carter Saxon who helped finance Keane in forming Del-Fi also claimed that he was never paid back. However, most of the sessions musicians had no trouble in being paid properly during the Del-Fi sessions. This may have been because the musicians' fees were well established since they belonged to the union. There is no clarification nor indication that contracts or agreements were offically signed or documented that spelled out the amounts due to others. According to the former attorney of Mrs. Valenzuela, Joseph Porter: "Ritchie was a minor when he entered into the recording and publishing contracts, some of which were never signed, others signed clearly a year after his death. I've found only one signature on any contract that was [actually] Ritchie's." He further went on to say that Keane had no right to sell or lease Valens' recordings (*if* he did sell them) during the ten-year gap, in the U.S. or to overseas companies. These recordings have been transferred and sold so many times that several people can claim ownership. Porter added, "I don't think anyone can stand up in a court of law and claim a clear title to Ritchie's masters, except for his estate."

Although he received payment for performances and appearances, there is some debate about whether Ritchie ever personally received a royalty for a record sale, other than the $1,000. Outside of the 1960 settlement and a suit of Dwyer Flying Service, the question of the Valens estate receiving the proper royalties from 1960 to the present, including overseas royalties, is clearly a legal matter that may never be resolved.

In recent years, two matters have been attended to. In 1975, Kemo Music, Valens' music publishers, sued rock group Led Zeppelin for re-titling Ritchie's "Ooh, My head" to "Boogie with

Stu." The issue was settled on July 28, 1978, out of court for a reported $130,000 plus future royalties of which Mrs. Valenzuela received a portion. In 1981, all the Del-Fi recordings were re-released under Rhino Records and reportedly an agreement was made between Keane and the Valens estate for future royalties. In the coming years, it remains to be seen when it comes time for copyright renewal whether all transferred interests to Ritchie's publishing and masters will revert to the Valens estate.

*   *   *

Chicano/Latino Rock and Valens' Influences

Ritchie Valens was never forgotten within the Chicano communities in the Southwest. There were some special attempts to keep his name and memory alive at least in Southern California. His recording of "La Bamba" opened the eyes of the music industry and made them aware that there was indeed a Latin-buying community. Ritchie was the essential beginning of a movement in rock music that remained unrecognized by the rest of the country and was hardly even defined by early rock historians until a few years ago. Chicano rock, also Latino rock, was the mixing of traditional Latin rhythms with rock and roll. It was performed by artists of Hispanic ancestry (in the case of Chicano rock, by those of Mexican background, though it may sometimes have included other Hispanics from the Southwest).

At the height of Ritchie's success, other Chicano artists were performing mostly around the Southern California area and, like Ritchie, were influenced by and performed Black-influenced rhythm and blues stylings of the likes of Little Richard, Larry Williams, Don and Dewey, Sam Cooke, and the Johnny Otis Show. Artists like Lil' Julian Herrera, who had a doo-wop local hit with "Lonely Lonely Nights" in 1956, still performed around town. Other artists in the post-Valens era, mostly from East L.A., like the Salas Brothers, Lil' Ray (who recorded for Del-Fi a cover of Ben E. King's hit "I Who Have Nothing"), the Velveteens, Rene and Ray, were clearly in the r 'n' b style of the Los Angeles area. After Ritchie's death, there was an immediate awareness of his style. Rocha recalled, "Some of the local boys started picking up from the Spanish guitar to the electric guitar. Guys were coming to me right and left wanting to be like Ritchie, imitating his songs. I tried to help them with the little musical knowledge I had about the guitar."

Strangely enough, the first performers to emerge from the Valens imitation/sound-alike phenomena, making recordings in the "Valens style," were not from the Los Angeles area. Chan Romero, a veteran performer around Billings, Montana, was the first. Don Redfield, a D.J. and a friend of Chan's heard that Keane was actively looking for a "Ritchie Valens sound-alike" and sent a tape to Keane. Romero was contacted and went to L.A. to cut his first single, "Hippy Hippy Shake," on Del Fi (DF 4119), April, 1959, just two months after Ritchie's death. Apparently, there was a concerted effort to keep the "Valens sound" intact: The same sessions musicians were used on the cuts with Barney Kessel on rhythm guitar, Irving Ashby on the double bass, Rene Hall on dan-electro and Earl Palmer on drums; Chan was on vocals and played lead guitar. He also played piano but not on the Del-Fi sessions. For all its initial intentions, "Hippy Hippy Shake" is an expression of Chan's very best in his own musical right. In his guitar work, Chan's breaks are very imitative of Ritchie's. However, Chan's vocal styling is unlike the Valens sound in that it is more intensely expressive and emotional. The reflective, often melancholy lyricism found in the Valens vocals is missing altogether in Romero's style. Though Chan Romero is more "soulful" than Ritchie, his style is traced more to a rural rockabilly influence rather than the more urbanized rhythm and blues. This element is brought out more strongly in Chan's follow-up recording, "My Little Ruby," in which the music is more likened to Anglo "hot-rod" instrumentals of the day. "Hippy Hippy Shake" and "My Little Ruby" became local hits, but did little on the national charts. "Hippy Hippy Shake" was released in England under Columbia (DB 4341), but made no impression there except on those who would become a group known as the Swinging Blue Jeans. They recorded their version of the song which became No. 2 on the English charts in February, 1964, with their Mersey beat and a guitar break that suspiciously resembled the "Valens/Romero" sound.

While in Los Angeles, Chan Romero stayed with Ritchie's family during the Del-Fi sessions. Eventually he also recorded on other labels—Living Legend, Challenge and Phillips—this time, employing his own stylings. When the Swinging Blue Jeans hit big with his song, Chan teamed up with former post-Holly Cricket Jerry Naylor to write more songs for the English group. Around the late 60's, Chan became a born-again Christian and started a recording studio for gospel music called Warrior Records in his home town of Billings. Today, he is still involved in this field, singing and writing for the group Faith, Hope and Charity.

Eddie Quinteros, the other notable "Valens stylist," hailed from Daly City, California, in the San Francisco area. Eddie started out with a Daly City band, the Rockateers, which was connected to Bobby Freeman, the creator and singer of the 1958 hit "Do You Wanna Dance." He may have come to the attention of Brent Records via Freeman, who was on Josie. Both companies were subsidiaries of Jubilee Records. In 1960, Quinteros recorded "Come Dance With Me" (Brent 7009), clearly in the Valens style. This song became a regional hit, especially in the California area, and made a few waves in areas with large Hispanic populations. Although he did not play guitar on the song, Quinteros openly admitted his influence from Valens. He went on to record three other songs, two more in the Valens style, "Slow Down Sandy/Lindy Lou" (Brent 7014), before going to Del-Fi in 1963 where he recorded "Pretty Baby I Love You" (DF 4156) with little success. Sometime before his contract with Brent, Eddie also recorded "Come On Little Girl" for M&K (102), possibly before getting into a Valens sound. Little else is known about that song.

Quinteros faded from the recording scene after Del-Fi, but Keane continued recording other lesser known artists with tints of Ritchie Valens in their styles, such as the Addrissi Brothers' "Cherrystone" (DF 4116) and Don and Dick's "Saving My Kisses/ Un Jarro" (DF 4120). These artists were non-Chicano in origin, but a Chicano group, the Carlos Brothers, recorded several songs with the same backing musicians Ritchie had had. The Carlos Brothers also did a re-recording of "La Bamba," utilizing the same backing track as Ritchie's version, this time adding horns and their vocals and editing out Ritchie's vocal but not his guitar playing! The success of this concept was best expressed by the buying public's avoidance of the recording altogether.

The first Los Angeles musician to admit influence from Ritchie Valens came from Hawthorne, California. Chris Montez, born Ezekil Montanez, also played guitar. One noticeable difference was that Chris patterned his musical stylings after Ritchie while Ritchie was alive. He even had the chance to meet Ritchie. Said Montez, "I had always admired Ritchie. I met him just before he died and was most impressed with his wonderful personality and vast musical knowledge. He was killed around the time I started singing (publicly) and it was a big blow to our community. I guess in a way I tried to fill the gap left by his passing."

Montez made his first recordings around 1960 for an unknown label, possibly under the name of Ezekil Montanez. These songs were recorded both in Spanish and English. Two of them, "Say You'll Marry Me/Rockin' Blues," are found on a rare German LP (Line Label). *Come Dance With Me* is a collection of Chicano rock featuring Valens, Romero and Quinteros, as well as Montez (under Montanez), and run-of-the-mill Anglo rockabilly songs. In 1961, Montez went to New York and came to the attention of Jim Lee while he was recording for Guaranteed Label. Lee had just formed a West Coast label, Monogram, and decided to push Montez and Kathy Young as his major artists. Young had a hit earlier in the fall of 1960 with "A Thousand Stars" on Indigo Records, another label of Lee's. Young had been a friend of Ritchie's and eventually she married John Maus of John and Judy fame. Montez' first recording for Monogram was "All You Had to Do" (Monogram 500) which was later re-recorded with Young (Monogram 517). His biggest hit was "Let's Dance" written by Jim Lee and released in July, 1962. It had become a top ten national hit. By that time, Chris had abandoned playing the guitar while singing, yet he remained faithful in his vocal stylings to the "Valens sound." In his album *Let's Dance,* ballads like "You're the One" strongly resemble Valens' "We Belong Together," and rockers like "No, No, No," "Chiquita Mía," "I Ran" and "Rockin' Blues" are examples of the Valens sound-alikes. Chris also recorded "In a Turkish Town," changing the name to "In an English Town" which was released on an English EP (London RE 1392). By 1965, Montez left Monogram to join up with Herb Alpert and A & M Records. Though not of Mexican ancestry, Alpert was influenced by Mexican *mariachi* music, yet none of that influence seeped into Montez' A & M recordings. His first record for them in 1966 was "Call Me," which showed clearly a pop mainstream vein with a slightly Latin tinge, an abandonment of rock and roll and alongside it the

"Valens sound." Montez went on to record in this style until he faded from the record scene. It is rumored that he is presently living somewhere in Simi Valley.

The period from 1958 through 1963 can be defined as the "first" period or wave of Chicano rock music. After 1963 and through 1966, outside of the local r 'n' b song stylists, one solo singer maintained the Chicano tradition and became a success— Trini López. López' guitar playing and backups, as expressed in his first hit, "If I Had a Hammer," are clearly in a Latin rock vein and bear strong resemblance to Valens' demos, yet oddly enough, the music industry relegated him to the then newly emerging "folk" wave that was hitting the charts. In addition, López hailed from Texas and leaned more toward claiming his influences from the so-called "Tex-Mex" tradition (in *rock*, not folk!).

A thorough discussion of the "Tex-Mex" traditions in rock and folk will be presented later in the chapter, but the years 1965 through 1968 can be characterized as the "second" period of Chicano rock music. This wave was made up of groups, both instrumental and vocal, and emanated not only from California (mostly the East L.A. area), but also from Texas. If there was any time that Chicano rock had a "golden" period, this was it for many of the songs hit the national charts and/or hit the top ten in other cities outside of the state of California. The "Valens sound" influenced many of these groups especially in the way they played and/or sang "La Bamba," by now considered a dance hall staple. However, another influence, carried over by Montez' "Let's Dance," was a crucial characteristic of several of these groups' sound: the introduction of the organ in a rock and roll band. The organ had previously appeared in late 50's songs such as "Born Too Late" by the Pony Tails and "The Happy Organ" played by Dave "Baby" Cortez, but the musical instrument did not feature strongly as a rock and roll instrument until "Let's Dance." A year later (1963), the Kingsmen, a rock band from Portland, Oregon, re-emphasized its use with their smash hit, "Louie, Louie." Their rendition of the old Richard Berry tune established the organ's place in rock 'n' roll. East L.A. (and later Texas) bands took the lead in using the organ in an ensemble. Ironically, several of the songs made famous by East L.A. bands such as "Farmer John" and "Whittier Blvd." by Thee Midniters were also covered by Northwest rock bands. It is a "chicken before the egg" concept of who influenced who, but the musical exchange via hit records between California and Texas Chicano bands and the Northwest is quite evident. Also, the organ continued to be the main featured instrument for such bands as Sam the Sham and the Pharoahs and the Sir Douglas Quintet, both from Texas, and ? and the Mysterians, a Texas-sounding band from Michigan.

The 60's history of the California Chicano bands originated at the Rainbow Gardens in Pomona, a night club where both Valens and Montez had performed in previous years. The Gardens served as an asset to introduce Latino/Chicano rock to a wider audience, especially with the TV production, "Stompin' at the Rainbow," hosted by L.A. D.J.'s such as Wink Martindale, Elliot Fields and Gene Weed. Producer Billy Cárdenas and Eddie Davis were other recording managers besides Keane responsible for bringing recognition to Chicano talent (with the recording labels of Faro, Lind and Ramparts). They worked closely with booking agent Candy Mendoza to bring the talents of r 'n' b influenced groups such as the Romanceers, the Velveteens, the Blendalls, Ronnie and the Pomona Casuals and the Mixtures, among others. Other important places where these groups performed in the mid-60's were the Paramount Ballroom, the Big Union Hall the legendary El Monte Legion Stadium.

By 1964, the sound of rock and roll had definitely changed. The British phenomenon of the Beatles was firmly rooted, and along with it, a distinctly British sound. As well, the dance craze earlier personified by the twist in the 1960 developed into other dance forms. These elements had considerable influence, as displayed by Ronnie and the Pomona Casuals' "I Wanna Do the Jerk," (who also recorded for Del-Fi). Cannibal and the Headhunters, originally from a housing project in East L.A., scored so well with their hit "Land of a Thousand Dances" that they were one of the opening acts of the Beatles U.S. Tour. Though not an instrument-playing group, they combined the backdrop sounds of the Eastside instrumental groups such as the Blendalls, the Premiers and Thee Midniters and applied them to Motown-Miracles/Temptations'-influenced harmonies and dance routines. From California, it was Cannibal and the Headhunters who emerged with national recognition.

Out of Texas came Sam the Sham and the Pharoahs who scored big with "Wooly Bully" in 1964 and subsequently with

"Lil' Red Riding Hood" in 1965. Though not entirely Chicano in make-up, Sam the Sham and the Pharoahs had the distinct sound that characterized the groups from East L.A., but with more of a "polished" finish. The same can also be said about the Sir Douglas Quintet in which only one member was Chicano (leader Doug Sham, though Anglo, was so highly acculturated to the Chicano experience that his friends referred to him as "Doug Saldaña"), but the sound was there in their hit "She's About A Mover." It is also there in "Ninety-six Tears" by ? and the Mysterians, a mostly Chicano band, oddly enough, from Michigan! However, the Mysterians' sound is closer to the polished Texas product than the more "earthy" sounding California band. In 1964, there was one other group from Texas that hit well with a record—Sunny and the Sunglows. They were more r 'n' b influenced which is apparent in their hit "Talk To Me."

By 1968, the "second period" began to wane as rock became more experimental and psychedelic. At the same time, there was a political consciousness gradually awakening among those of Mexican heritage, best expressed by 1970 with the Chicano Moratorium and the school walkouts in L.A. for better education. There came a "third period" of Chicano music, headed by such groups as Santana and El Chicano.

El Chicano made national waves in 1970 with their hit "Viva Tirado," an instrumental with a heavier influence from Afro-Latin elements. Most of their music stemmed from these origins and for that time, along with the more well known Santana, the earlier sounds of the 50's and 60's, including that of Ritchie Valens, were virtually forgotten. El Chicano, as indicated by their name, seemed to carry more of a socio-political stance in their music, perhaps what was sorely needed to express to the rest of the world that they were *there*—that they existed musically as a visible entity. On the other hand, Santana was not as socio-politically oriented, yet their aggressively hard rock/Afro-Latin sound, which often employed traditional Latin instruments such as congas, timbales, cowbell, maracas and claves, made people beyond the Hispanic community sit up and take notice. Songs of theirs such as "Black Magic Woman" and "You Better Change Your Evil Ways" seemed more Afro-Cuban/Latin rather than definably "Chicano." The two groups' ethnic makeups were mostly other Hispanics and Blacks. There were other Chicano groups—Azteca and Malo—but El Chicano and Santana made the national waves. Santana's sound fitted in well with the hard rock of the day, but as the 70's mellowed out, so did both Santana and El Chicano.

With the 70's and into the 80's comes the possibility of a "fourth period" or wave of Chicano music that seems to combine elements from all three previous movements, and consists of both innovation and revivalism. The 70's were low-keyed for groups, however, one solo singer stood out among the rest: Freddy Fender. Coming from Texas, his style has been linked to something defined as "Tex-Mex R&B," though his sales are primarily in the country-western market. Fender had been around longer than Valens, but due to struggling complexities within his own life, he did not break big until meeting up with Huey Meaux, a Houston producer who also worked with the Sir Douglas Quintet. Fender revived a song he recorded in 1959, "Wasted Days and Wasted Nights," which became a smash on the country charts. He also continued his success with "Before the Next Teardrop Falls" (both songs recorded around 1975-76). Fender earned the name "El Bebop Kid" by reviving old rhythm and blues and rock and roll standards with a country flare, including Valens' "Donna." He was influenced by the music of the 50's in its entirety rather than by any specific individuals.

Within the last eight years, new Chicano groups from the California area have sprung up within the new wave/punk rock movements. Groups like the Plugz, Mestizo and the Brat are continually performing, this time, with a conscious awareness of the Valens legacy. Songs like "La Bamba" and "Come On, Let's Go" are likely to be found in their repertoires. Another group, Tierra, which performs in the style of El Chicano, some of whose members go back to the Eastside groups, occasionally performs Valens tunes.

However, there is one group which stands out among them all. Within the last three years, this group, Los Lobos, has had an impact that transcends the original Valens sensation. Coming from East L.A., David Hidalgo, César Rosas, Conrad Lozano, Luis Pérez and Steve Berlin who make up the group, had been playing for ten years straight before making it big with the hit "Will the Wolf Survive." They not only play but combine the essence of the Valens sound with other Chicano-influenced rock sounds; in addition, they also go back to traditional Mexican folkloric roots of norteña and mariachi musics.

Ken Tucker, music critic for the *Philadelphia Inquirer*, who helped get Los Lobos national recognition, ties them in with the Valens perspective: "Ritchie Valens [was] a pioneering influence in rock and roll, someone who came along at the same time as Chuck Berry, Little Richard, etc., and he was the only Latino performer to make that kind of impact in pop music at the time. Since then, it's as if a whole people have been closed out of that kind of music, that the music business had very consciously said, 'That's not commercial!' Carlos Santana came in from a whole different direction, on his own terms, but through a whole different approach to rock guitar. But you can see that line of history being re-connected with Los Lobos which is very exciting and makes the music much richer."

"We realize that Ritchie Valens was the greatest around," says David Hidalgo. "Here, this guy was only seventeen years old. Now, we know his family and they are real nice folks." Hidalgo also mentioned that Los Lobos plays "Donna," "La Bamba," have already recorded, "Come On, Let's Go," and "fool around" with "That's My Little Suzie" and "In A Turkish Town." Los Lobos have been chosen to do the background music for the movie, *La Bamba* with Hidalgo doing the Valens solos.

Another question arises about how much Ritchie Valens influenced non-Chicano artists. Lester Bangs' statement of "La Bamba" being the heart of all protopunk garage-band sounds can be interpreted to mean that anyone who had recorded or played "La Bamba" was essentially aware of the Valens version for almost always, the beginning guitar riff characterized in the Valens version was there. There were other songs that seemed to be takeoffs from the melody of "La Bamba": "Juarez Town" by Johnny Burnette, "Twist and Shout" by the Isley Brothers (later covered by the Beatles), "Moulty" by the Barbarians and, of course, "Louie, Louie" by the Kingsmen. The post-Holly Crickets did an English version called "(They Call Her) La Bamba." "Donna" tended to be recorded by artists with a more pop appeal such as Johnny Crawford and Donny Osmond. All other Valens tunes were virtually forgotten or stuck away in a singer's lesser known LP such as Ronnie Hawkins' version of "Come On, Let's Go," released in the mid-60's. By that time, most of the other Valens songs were not easily available. It was not until Led Zeppelin's "Boogie with Stu," a.k.a., "Ooh, My Head," in 1975 that another Valens song was apparent. In 1978, other Valens songs surfaced through another non-Chicano group, the Ramones, and their recordings of "Come On, Let's Go" (sung with the Paley Brothers) and "Blitzkrieg Bop," all from the movie soundtrack for *Rock and Roll High School*. It can also be said that the Ramones continued to bring the Valens sound to the forefront.

Another more recent group from Texas contributes elements that may hearken back to Ritchie Valens, adding a predominantly 60's organ sound, as well as applying rhythms from the more traditional "border" music. This combination of sounds is expressed by none other than Joe "King" Carrasco and his backup band. Although Carrasco is not Chicano, his music reflects a definite Texas Chicano sound, bringing in the elements of the Sir Douglas Quintet and Sam the Sham, and he occasionally sings songs partially in Spanish such as "Buena" and "Caca de Vaca."

One more question arises as to the relationship of the Valens sound to the term "Tex-Mex." This term has been used and abused to define diverse kinds of rock and roll, from Buddy Holly or Duane Eddy to the Sir Douglas Quintet. In its traditional definition, "Tex-Mex" refers to the *border* music (popular music, stemming from Mexican folk origins, from the "norteña" or northern states of Mexico), played by the Mexican-American community along the south Texas border. Sir Douglas Quintet's "She's About A Mover" uses the rhythmic sequences found in the traditional "Tex-Mex," as does their recently revived material and the farfisa-dominated rocking music of Joe "King" Carrasco.

Another concept of "Tex-Mex" refers to the rock and roll music of Texas/New Mexico, specifically to Norman Petty's recording studios, from the sounds of Buddy Holly and the Crickets to Buddy Knox and the Rhythm Orchids, the post-Holly Crickets and the Fireballs. A description was attempted by Holly biographer David Laing, stating "Tex-Mex" as "barrages of chords, with a powerful electric tone . . . a unique metallic sound where each chord echoes into the next." This description only included Holly's music (it may be added that Holly's melodic lines as well as chords echoed into the next!), but is typical of Valens' music *and* ultimately of Chuck Berry and Bo Diddley! Bob Keane said, "After I saw 'The Buddy Holly Story,' I realized, whether he knew it or not, that Ritchie had a lot of Buddy Holly stuff."

At face value, this is incorrect. From what others recalled, friends and musicians alike, Ritchie never played Holly's music nor did he play that much rockabilly, outside of an occasional Elvis, Everly Brothers and, at a later date, Eddie Cochran. However, in a broad and perhaps very general perspective, a similarity can be drawn in the use of simple musical elements, such as repetitive phrases in vocal or guitar playing that creates a mesmerizing effect. This definition may be too broad for it would also have to include the likes of Duane Eddy's instrumentals like "Rebel Rouser" and "Forty Miles of Bad Road," or the Champs' "Tequila," or "Ninety-Six Tears" by the Mysterians, "Louie, Louie" by the Kingsmen, and a host of others who happened to have been influenced by those from the Southwest or West Coast. In the context of Texas and New Mexico, the Valens sound could hardly be called "Tex-Mex."

There is yet another kind of "Tex-Mex": "Tex-Mex R&B," whose roots are neither Texas or Mexican, rather Louisiana and Black, with sprinklings of Cajun and country-western. The "Tex-Mex R&B" appellation stuck because of the *performers* such as Freddy Fender and Sunny and the Sunglows. But its characteristic, slow ballad-type songs developed out of a Louisiana rock scene from Anglo performers singing r 'n' b: Jimmy Clanton ("Just A Dream"), Phil Phillips ("Sea of Love"), Bruce Channel ("Hey, Baby"), and Paul and Paula ("Hey, Paula"). The scene developed around the late 50's and early 60's; its earlier and rhythmically faster roots in the form of Little Richard and Fats Domino stemmed from Louisiana and directly made their way via residency and recording sessions into the Los Angeles studios of Specialty and Imperial where southern Californians picked it up firsthand. Therefore, in listening to the "Tex-Mex R&B" standards, one can hear that the ballads of Valens such as "Donna" and "We Belong Together" stylistically share similar roots.

The capsule history of the Chicano/Latino rock scene points to one fact: Were it not for "Donna," "La Bamba," and to a lesser extent, "Come On, Let's Go," in essence, were it not for Ritchie Valens, this musical scene may have turned in a totally different direction which may have lessened the impact of the Latin background as a substantial musical element.

10

POSTSCRIPTS

1. The Aftermath

The story of Ritchie Valens was a happy story that had an untimely tragic ending. It should never be taken in the same way as the story of Buddy Holly. It is not to say that Holly's death was not tragic but there is an underlining note of memorable perception. Holly had slightly more time to accomplish his goals (the same could also be said of Ritchie's other associate, Eddie Cochran), and there was a concerted effort on the part of manager, family, friends and fans to perpetuate his memory, however controversial the means may have been. In the case of Valens, a shallow effort to preserve his memory was made, but the overall shock of the tragedy combined with cultural and legal complexities among family, manager and friends was far more overwhelming than what was visible to the public.

The fame that Ritchie won had been a surprise to his family and his older brother and mother were just beginning to grasp Ritchie's popularity at the time of the plane crash. None of his immediate family were musicians nor did they have any inklings of the workings of show business, yet Ritchie's pursuits were unanimously condoned. With Ritchie, there was an eager interest to discover as quickly as humanly possible, but not without strong misgivings. According to Morales, he once asked Ritchie, after he appeared on "The Dick Clark Show" and crowds of teenagers started coming to the house, how he felt about all of it. Ritchie replied, "It's happening too fast. It's too confusing." Yet knowing that music was his life, he was determined to go forth and learn as much as he could about that new and wonderful thing known as rock and roll. Since his death and until recently, within the past five years, the family's memories of Ritchie have been deliberately retained as reticent remembrances, even among each other, rather than revealing anything openly to the public. The shocking circumstances of the death, not to mention legal disputes over royalties, did not help any in keeping Ritchie's memory in a more positive light.

Bob Keane and Del-Fi records may have done all they could in keeping the Valens legacy alive while contesting with serious legal disputes, but the additional factors of possible inexperience on the part of Del-Fi, a relatively small and independent label in the face of stronger "indie" recording companies, and the sudden discontinuation of the Ritchie Valens Memorial Club (headed by a former secretary who to this day refuses to discuss her relationship to Keane, Del-Fi and the Club) also contributed to the waning memory of Ritchie Valens. One more item — the element of racism — cannot be ruled out. It must be remembered that the *majority* of fans, even those of Mexican heritage, did not know Ritchie was of Mexican descent until well into the 60's! Yet, would Ritchie have been remembered more had he been Anglo? To whatever extent it may be argued in respect to the Valens legacy, an *attitude* does exist toward those of American-Mexican background.

Above it all, however, there is one highlight — Ritchie was *never* forgotten by the general Mexican-American community, especially in California, even though his recordings were few and often inaccessible. At present, Ritchie's recognition is becoming far more apparent because he was essentially the first to effectively combine rock with a Latin/Chicano rhythm. In respect to the Anglo world, it has happened because of the attention which has focused on Buddy Holly and a curiosity to discover just who were the other two singers who died in the same crash with him. For the past five years, it has been mostly Anglo writers who have taken the initiative to restore Ritchie's memory.

Danny Valdez, one of the major actors in the film *Zoot Suit*, who is currently developing a movie on Ritchie's life, is an ardent fan intrigued by the innocent yet intense style of Valens' music. He said, "The injustice is that the audience never knew who Ritchie was, where he came from or what shaped him. He is an inspirational story to youth, the kid on the porch, *all* kids on the porch, be they black, brown or whatever. You have the settlement of a migrant family in Pacoima, epitomizing the migration of manual labor — working class people — to the cities. You have that innocence of youth, that openness we all felt when we were teenagers."

Since 1962, there have been several attempts to bring Ritchie's story to the screen, more so since 1978 with the release of *The Buddy Holly Story.* Valdez' most recent attempts have been in collaboration with efforts by Bob Morales to make the possibility of a film production for the first time a reality. This project has culminated in the form of a movie titled *La Bamba,* for which Luis Valdez is the director, brother Danny the associate producer, and Taylor Hackford of *An Officer and A Gentleman* and *White Nights* fame the producer. The film, starring Lou Diamond Phillips as Valens, will be distributed through Columbia Pictures and is scheduled to be released in the summer of 1987. This movie is the most promising effort to date. As well, others are looking at a possible documentary of Ritchie's life for TV and still others are seeking film clips or kinescopes which show Ritchie on and off stage. All these inquiries are pointing to the preservation of the memory of a unique seventeen-year-old in a more profound way than ever before.

Had Ritchie lived, there is no doubt that he would have been famous, merely judging by the unique music he produced. Whether Del-Fi's fate would have changed is another debatable issue. Even had Ritchie not always made it to the "top ten," he still would have been renowned among local Californians and the Latino community. What would have happened had Ritchie hooked up with other California notables such as the Beach Boys or Phil Spector is left to the realms of the imagination.

It is folly to think that Ritchie would have been hailed as "the next Elvis," yet, he would've had something special of his own going for him. With the few recordings he did, so much could be perceived in them that was uniquely his own. Fortunately, by the current activities, it seems apparent that unlike other past notables in music and the arts, it won't take fifty or more years to discover who Ritchie Valens was. His story is common yet profoundly unique, the most important element being that he was never forgotten by his own people. As long as there is a Chicano people, there will always be a Ritchie Valens.

2. *La Bamba:* A Review

La Bamba. (New Visions Production) (distr. Columbia Pictures) (1987)

Written and directed by Luis Valdez; produced by Taylor Hackford and Bill Borden; original music by Carlos Santana and Miles Goodman. (Valens' songs sung by David Hidalgo of Los Lobos.)

La Bamba stars Esai Morales (as Robert Morales, Ritchie's older brother); Rosana DeSoto (as Ritchie's mother, Connie Valenzuela); Elizabeth Peña (as Rosie Morales, Bobby's wife); Joe Pantoliano as Bob Keene; and introducing Lou Diamond Phillips as Ritchie Valens.

As of this writing, I have only seen *La Bamba* once. I plan to see it again and again. Notwithstanding my affiliations with Valens and his music, I feel this is one of the most enjoyable films to come along in quite a few years. The cinematography is superb, especially in capturing the golden California hills. The acting is great on the parts of both the lead and the minor characters, and there are solid, strong female roles, with DeSoto's performance as Ritchie's mother high among them. There are memorable classic scenes and some good lines. The humor for the most part is genuine, and there are cameo appearances by musicians such as Los Lobos and by members of Ritchie's immediate family. (Irma Balcorta, Ritchie's sister, plays a "farmworker"; her daughter Gloria plays "Little Irma"; younger brother Mario Ramírez' baby plays "Little Mario," and there is a shot of Ritchie's real mother in the "home movie" sequence.)

However, there is a dilemma, and it arises from two basic inquiries: Why did New Visions decide to go along with a story line loosely based on Valens' life, and why did most of the immediate family agree to this fictionalized account?

The answer to the first question may be that Luis Valdez was seeking to present the "legend" of Ritchie Valens by taking certain incidents from Valens' life and elaborating on them, as seems to be the case with most Hollywood-based biographies. By creating this "legend" of Valens, Valdez could maintain the key points of Ritchie's life and music and, at the same time, safeguard the privacy of the immediate family. This may account for the family's participation in *La Bamba.*

There was a story to tell solely about Ritchie (as my book has hoped to illustrate), but the film company was more attracted to the "colorful" character of his older brother, Bob. The writers and producers of *La Bamba* recognized the potential for a "Cain and Abel" story in the relationship of Bob and Ritchie. From my perspective, I am not certain how intense the conflicts were between Bob and Ritchie, but I assume they have been embellished to suit the needs of the screenplay. Other factors that form the basis of this film are far more urgent: Ritchie was *never* a farmworker or migrant laborer; he did not go to Tijuana with his brother nor meet a *curandero* who gave him an amulet made of snake skin; and he never sang Buddy Holly tunes in a country/ western bar. Lou Diamond Phillips, who plays Valens, is the opposite, physically, of Ritchie Valens. Moreover, his performance style is unlike Valens' troubadour-style stage presentations. Phillips imitates the more commonplace gyrations associated with many rockabilly artists of the day. His acting is excellent, but his portrayal of Valens as the happy-go-lucky, good-humored, and musically gifted youth that he was does not always come through. There is a scene of Ritchie recording "Come On, Let's Go"—*without* his guitar! (Throughout the film, we constantly see "Ritchie" with a guitar, making this scene quite unlikely.) Also, the roles of his aunt and uncle, his friends, and the sessions musicians have been minimized.

There is an attempt to adhere to certain items associated with Ritchie, e.g., the white sweater (with the black and blue piping) worn on the first album, the blue satin shirt with the black vest and pants, the green and white electric guitar and small amplifier Ritchie used to carry, and a standard photo of Ritchie which was remade with Phillips' face (this is seen in the background of one of the scenes of the movie).

The screenplay does show basic events that happened in Ritchie's life, but they seem to revolve around other incidents—e.g., "Ritchie's nightmares," or Bob's quest to be a cartoonist—that can be defined as typical Hollywood "dramatic license." After viewing *La Bamba*, I asked several people if it bothered them that what they saw on the screen was not all that accurate, to which most of them replied, "Well, that's Hollywood for you!"

I truly appreciate Luis Valdez for writing a screenplay about Ritchie Valens. I know this film will boost the long-overdue popularity of Valens. I also know that from this film the public's perception of Ritchie Valens' character may be permanently misguided. As long as there is an awareness on the part of the public that *La Bamba* is indeed a "legend" on screen, not unlike the "legend" that was created in celluloid about Buddy Holly, then I can forsee considerable success with the movie and a guaranteed special place for Ritchie Valens in the history of early rock and roll.

3. Los Lobos and Ritchie Valens

Special mention should be made of the East L.A. rock group Los Lobos and their affiliation with Ritchie Valens.

In the phases of Chicano/Latino rock, Los Lobos represents the "fifth" stage of that music's history, because they have pulled the previous four periods together in a way that no other group has. In the eyes of some rock critics, outside of the very few one-hit exceptions such as Thee Midniters, Sam the Sham, and ? and the Mysterians, Los Lobos is the only successful rock act of Chicano/Mexicano background since Ritchie Valens to come along and combine Mexican musical elements with rock and roll! Ironically, they have recorded the soundtrack for *La Bamba*, the movie of Valens' life and music. David Hidalgo, one of the lead vocals/composer and guitarist/accordianist for the band, indicated that from the beginning, the Valenzuela family wanted them to do the soundtrack. Said Hidalgo, "We feel real close [to the family] when we do [Ritchie's] music. He was a gifted young man." It was not until quite late (namely ten or so years ago) that Hidalgo was aware that Ritchie was only seventeen when he died, although he had most of Ritchie's records (in singles, because he could not find any albums). Hidalgo's role in *La Bamba* can be summed up in a statement he recently made to *Guitar Player:* "It took us [Los Lobos] a while to figure out what was going on in the original [Valens] records. Like 'Donna,' I think what they did was mike the guitar amp, and then mike the [guitar] strings. The amp is real bassy and muffled-sounding, filling up the track, while they put some slap on the other mike, on the [guitar] strings. We tried it and it came out just like the record! 'Okay, man. Let's go home,' we said. 'This is scary!'" Hidalgo did Ritchie's vocals in the movie, but the vocal tracks were speeded up a little to sound more like Valens. He also played drums on the Valens version of the Little Richard song "Rip It Up" because it was one of his favorite Earl Palmer [drummer for both Little

Richard and Ritchie Valens] songs. One of the guitars he used for the soundtrack was a long-neck dan-electro six-string bass, not unlike the dan-electro employed in most of Valens' tunes.

When I first met César Rosas, the other lead guitarist and vocalist of the group, he had just purchased a new electric guitar, and the first song he played on it was Ritchie's "Rockin' All Night." To me, he represents many in the Chicano/Latino community with respect to Valens. He had heard of Ritchie Valens, and his songs "Donna/La Bamba," but that was the extent of it, until a few years ago. His specialty was the rock music of the late 60's/early 70's. "It was a whole different thing," said Rosas. "The world wasn't into that stuff. We have always heard of Ritchie, but there weren't any records available."

Rosas always had the highest respect for Valens' music. In respect to *La Bamba*, Rosas said, "The movie was really a lot of hard work and headaches, but, at the same time, it was an honor to be in it. We worked on the music projects for months, from March [1986] until the end of the year." Los Lobos was so intent on getting the accurate sound of the original Valens songs that they would go back and re-cut the songs if they were not quite right.

The soundtrack album of *La Bamba* is due to be released in June 1987, a month before the July release of the movie, and it just may determine whether a revival of the original Valens songs will be in order before long.

11

BIBLIOGRAPHY

Books

Elson, Howard, and John Brunton. *Whatever Happened to . . . ?* New York: Proteus Publishing, 1981. 150.

Gerjerstam, Claes af. *Popular Music in Mexico.* Albuquerque, NM: University of New Mexico Press, 1976. 140.

Gillett, Charlie. *The Sound of the City: The Rise of Rock and Roll.* New York: Outerbridge and Dienstfrey, 1970. 128. New York: Dell Laurel Edition, 1972.

Goldrosen, John. *The Buddy Holly Story.* New York, London, Tokyo: Quick Fox Press, 1979. (Previously published in 1975 by Bowling Green University Popular Press as *Buddy Holly: His Life and Music.*)

Griggs, Bill, and Jim Black. *Buddy Holly: A Collector's Guide.* Sheboygan, WI: Red Wax Publishers, 1983. P. 84: U.S. Discography of Ritchie Valens.

Jones, Leroi. *Blues People.* New York: William Morrow & Co., 1963.

Liang, David. *Buddy Holly.* New York: Collier Books, 1971.

Marchbank, Pearce, and Miles *The Illustrated Rock Almanac.* New York & London: Paddington Press, Ltd., 1977.

Marsh, David, and Kevin Stein. *The Rolling Stone Book of Rock Lists.* New York: Dell/Rolling Stone Press, 1981.

Miller, Jim, ed. *The Rolling Stone Illustrated History of Rock 'n Roll.* New York: Rolling Stone Press, 1976, 1980. (Contains Lester Bangs' article on "Proto-punk," p. 261, in which Valens is credited as one of the originators of "punk" rock.)

Nite, Norm M. *Rock On: The Illustrated Encyclopedia of Rock 'n Roll.* New York: Popular Library (Thomas Y. Crowell), 1974, 1977. Vol. I.

Oliver, Paul. *Savannah Syncopators: African Retention in the Blues.* New York: Stein & Day, 1970, 1974.

Palmer, Robert. *Baby, That Was Rock 'n Roll: The Legendary Leiber & Stoller.* New York & London: Harcourt Brace Jovanovich (Harvest Books), 1978.

———. *A Tale of Two Cities: Memphis Rock and New Orleans Roll.* I.S.A.M. Monograph No. 12. New York: Institute for Studies in American Music, School of Performing Arts, Brooklyn College of the City University of New York, 1979.

Pollack, Bruce. *When Rock Was Young.* New York: Holt, Rinehart & Winston, 1981. 25, 31.

Propes, Steve. *Those Oldies But Goodies.* New York: Collier Books, 1973. 178-9.

Roxon, Lillian. *Lillian Roxon's Rock Encyclopedia.* New York: Grosset & Dunlap (Tempo Books), 1969, 1971, 1974. 504-5.

Shaw, Arnold. *Honkers and Shouters: The Golden Years of Rhythm & Blues.* New York: Collier Books, 1978. 265, 523.

Stambler, Irwin. *Encyclopedia of Pop, Rock and Soul.* New York: St. Martin's Press; London: St. James' Press, 1974, 1977. 530.

Wood, Graham. *An A–Z of Rock 'n Roll.* London: Studio Vista, 1971. 66, 107-8.

York, William. *Who's Who in Rock Music.* Seattle: Atomic Press, 1978. 241.

Articles

Aragon, Helen. "Tenth Anniversary of Tragedy Over Pacoima." *The Sun Day* (San Fernando Valley), Jan. 15, 1967: 1, 3.

Baker, Bob. "Ritchie Valens' Song Still Heard in Pacoima." *L.A. Times*, Feb. 2, 1984: 2-7.

Bangs, Lester. "Ritchie Valens in Concert at Pacoima Jr. High." *Rolling Stone*, July 9, 1970: 42.

Barrios, Greg. "Ritchie Valens: The First Chicano Rock 'n Roller." *Low Rider*, September 1981: 62-5.

Beale, Lewis. "'La Bamba,' Ritchie Valens Story, A Labor of Love and a Tribute to Hispanic Culture." *L.A. Life, Daily News*, August 15, 1986: cover, 8-9.

Beck, Roger, and Paul Weeks. "Story of a Dead Rock 'n Roll Star—Own Song Swept Valens to Fame." *L.A. Evening Mirror News*, Feb. 4, 1959: 1, 3.

Curtis, Jack. "Singer Had It Made at 17—Then, Sudden Death." *The Arizona Republic* (Phoenix), Feb. 5, 1959: 34.

Dallas, Karl. "They Died Young." *The History of Rock*, Vol. 1, No. 10 (1982): 194-5.

Dawson, Jim. "Ritchie Valens, The Lost Chicano." *L.A. Weekly*, March 15, 1979: 22.

———. "Ritchie Valens." *L.A. Times Calendar*, Feb. 3, 1980: 1, 100-1.

———. "The Story of L.A.'s *Other* Legend Named Valenzuela." *L.A. Herald-Examiner, Weekend Friday*, Sept. 4, 1981: 26.

Denisoff, R. Serge. "Waylon Jennings' 'The Last Tour': A New Journalism Approach." *Journal of Popular Culture*, Spring 1980: 663-71.

Forte, Dan. "Los Lobos: Tex-Mex Rock from East L.A." *Guitar Player*, Feb. 1987: 70-94.

Gains, Jim. "Fair Play for Ritchie." *New Record Mirror*, June 29, 1963: 6.

"The Girl Ritchie Left Behind." *16 Magazine*, July 1959: 26-28.

Goodwin, Keith. "They Died Too Soon." *New Musical Express*, Feb. 5, 1960: n. pag.

Gore, Robert J. "Beach Boys Booked at Queen Mary." *L.A. Times*, June 26, 1981: sec. VI.

Hansen, Barret. "The Tex-Mex Story" (History of the Southwest Scene). *Hit Parader*, Sept. 1968: 22-24, 52.

Hawkins, Martin. "Ritchie Valens." *The History of Rock*, Vol. 1, No. 10 (1982): 196-97.

Heatley, Michael. "Not Fade Away." *The History of Rock*. Vol. 1, No. 10 (1982): 181-83.

Hoffman, Jim. "We Belong Together." *Photoplay*, May 1959: 64-65, 84-86.

Larkin, Lou. "Why Did They Have to Die?" *Motion Picture*, May 1959: 50, 51, 79-80.

Lerner, Michael J. "Los Lobos: Born in East L.A." *Newsweek*, Feb. 23, 1987.

Lungstrum, Alan. "Ritchie Valens." *Rock and Roll Legends*, No. 4 (1983): 4-13.

Marcus, Griel. "(Records)." (On Holly and Valens,) *Rolling Stone*, June 28, 1969: 36.

"Meet Ritchie's 'Donna,'" *Teen Magazine*, May 1959: 19-21.

Meltsir (Harmetz), Aljean. "Portrait of a Family in Grief." *Motion Picture*, May 1959: 52-53, 72.

Myers, David, ed. "The Life and Death of Ritchie Valens." *Modern Screen* , May 1959: n. pag. (7 pp. text & illus.).

Nash, Bonnie. "The Night I Sang With Ritchie Valens," (as told by Bonnie Nash). *Dig Magazine*, April 1959: 34-35

Parker, Richard. "Wasted Days and Wasted Nights—An Overview of Tex-Mex R & B." *Goldmine*, July 1981: 8.

Phillip, Simon. "The Ritchie Valens Story." *Red Hot*, No. 2 (date unknown, but printed in the 1960's), 4 pp.

———. "Let's Dance the Hippy Hippy Shake: The Chicano Rock Scene After Valens." *Red Hot*, No. 3 (date unknown, but printed in the 1960's), 2 pp.

"Radio Review with Ritchie Valens." *Rock 'n Roll Songs*, Vol. 4, No. 17 (May 1959): 7.

"The Ritchie Valens Story." Printed in a fan magazine, title unknown, c. 1959.

Rodríguez, Luis. "The History of the Eastside Sound, Pt. 1." *L.A. Weekly*, August 1-7, 1980: 56-57.

———. "The History of the Eastside Sound, Pt. 2." *L.A. Weekly*, Aug. 15-21, 1980: 56, 58.

Russell, Wayne. "Rockabilly Profile: Chan Romero: From 'Hippy Hippy Shake' To God." *Goldmine*, October 1983: 206.

Samuelson, Dave. "The Music Shop: A Videography," (Rock Videophile's File). *Goldmine*, October 1983: 95.

Scott, Tony. "Leave Him to Heaven . . . and Ricky Valance [sic]." Article independently printed. Date of publication unknown, but in the 1960's.

Shock, Joyce. "Wonderful Sound—Reviews of 'Come On, Let's Go,' 'Donna,' and 'La Bamba,'" *Record Mirror*, Oct. 25, 1950, and Feb. 21, 1959.

Spencer, Dee. "When He Died, We Died, Too," (Star Personals). *Movie Life*, June 1959: 55-57.

"The Story Behind the Ritchie Valens Album." Independently released article through Del-Fi Records, n.d. 4 pp.

Tepper, Ron. "Buddy Bregman Will Introduce New 'Music Shop' Show in Color Tonight." *L.A. Times TV Section*, Jan. 11, 1959: 7.

"Tigerville Singing Star Makes Headlines." *Whirlwind* (San Fernando High School), Nov. 14, 1958.

12

DISCOGRAPHY

All recordings are listed by label, number, song or EP/LP title(s) and contents, date released or appeared on *Billboard*, and country of release. The author wishes to acknowledge Ragnar Ebsen and Gerd Muesfeldt for their assistance in compiling this discography.

Singles (45's and/or 78's)

Label	No.	Title (Contents)	Date	Country
Del-Fi	4106	Come On, Let's Go/Framed	9/13/58	USA
Pye-Int.	7N 25000[1]	Come On, Let's Go/Dooby Dooby Wah	11/58	UK
Metronome	B 1332	Come On, Let's Go/Dooby Dooby Wah	1959	West Ger./Denmark
Del-Fi	4110	Donna/La Bamba	11/17/58	USA
London	HL 8803	Donna/La Bamba	2/59	UK
Polydor	NH 66910	Donna/La Bamba	5/59	West Ger.
Del-Fi	4111[2]	Fast Freight/Big Baby Blues	12/58	USA

---

[1]This was the first Valens release in Great Britain and also the first recording of the Pye International series.

[2]This instrumental was initially released under the name "Arvee Allens." It was re-released in early 1959 under Valens' own name.

Label	No.	Title (Contents)	Date	Country
Del-Fi	4114	That's My Little Suzie/In a Turkish Town	4/4/59	USA
London	HL 8886	That's My Little Suzie/Bluebirds Over the Mountain	6/59	UK
Del-Fi	4117	Little Girl/We Belong Together	7/13/59	USA
Polydor	NH 66918	Ooh, My Head/Little Girl	6/59	West Ger.
Del-Fi	4128	Stay Beside Me/We Belong Together	10/59	USA
Del-Fi	4133	Paddiwack Song/Cry, Cry, Cry	mid-1960	USA
Heliodor	43 5119	Donna/La Bamba	1960	West Ger.
London	HL 9494	Ooh, My Head/La Bamba	1/62	UK
Sue	WI 4011	Donna/La Bamba	5/66	UK
President	PT 126	Donna/La Bamba	2/67	UK
Kasey	7040	La Bamba/Donna	mid-60's?	USA
Goldies	45 D-2626	Donna/We Belong Together	late 60's/early 70's?	U.S.A.
Goldies	45 D-2627	La Bamba/Bluebirds Over the Mountain	late 60's/early 70's?	U.S.A.
MCA	101 796-100	Donna/La Bamba	1979/1980?	West Ger.
President	12 242 AT	Donna/La Bamba	1972	West Ger.
Ariola	19 626 AT	Donna/La Bamba	mid-60's	West Ger.
Trip	TRS 64	Donna/La Bamba	late 60's	USA
Eric	139	Donna/La Bamba (stereo)	?	USA
Lost Nite	LN-201	Donna/La Bamba	late 60's?	USA
Old Gold	OG 9029	Donna/La Bamba	4/79	USA
London	HLR 10571	La Bamba/Come On, Let's Go/That's My Little Suzie	7/79	UK
Creole	CR 215	Donna/La Bamba (reverse by Chris Montez)	12/80	UK
London	FLX 3103	Donna/La Bamba	?	Holland
London	FLX 3117	That's My Little Suzie/Ooh, My Head (picture cover)	?	Holland
Bellaphon	100.07.243	La Bamba/Let's Dance (Chris Montez)	11/83	West Ger.

EP's (45's)

Label	No.	Title (Contents)	Date	Country
Del-Fi	101	Ritchie Valens: Donna/La Bamba/We Belong Together/Framed	1959	USA
Del-Fi	PR-1	(same EP as 101, but promo pressing)	1959	USA
Del-Fi	111	Ritchie Valens Sings: Come On, Let's Go/Donna/Bluebirds Over the Mt./Hi-Tone	1959	USA
London	RE 1232	Ritchie Valens: That's My Little Suzie/Ooh, My Head/Bluebirds Over the Mt./We Belong Together	9/59	UK
London	HLR 10571	Ritchie Valens: That's My Little Suzie/Come On, Let's Go/La Bamba	1975/76?	UK
Polydor	EPH 21 901	The Ritchie Valens Story: Donna/La Bamba/That's My Little Suzie/In a Turkish Town	6/59	West Ger.
Polydor	21 901 EPH	As above—cover information written in Spanish.	1959	Spain
Polydor	EPH 21 904	More Ritchie Valens: Stay Beside Me/Little Girl/Ooh, My Head/Framed	12/59	West Ger.
Decca-London	RE 10.174 EP	Donna/Cry,Cry,Cry/La Bamba/Come On, Let's Go	1960's?	France
Sonet	SVP 6055	Contents unknown.	?	Sweden
Sonet	SXP 6056	Contents unknown.	?	Sweden
Rocket '88	REP-002	The Great Tragedy (bootleg): Rock Little Donna/Let's Rock & Roll	1972/73?	Australia
President	05-19 7640	Ritchie Valens: Donna/La Bamba/In a Turkish Town/Come On, Let's Go	early 70's?	UK
Line	LS 1075 AC	Promo EP, one selection by Valens: That's My Little Suzie (six selections, total)	6/82	West Ger.

LP's (33's)

Albums with their contents from the United States, Canada, and United Kingdom; also various other European and Australian releases, including bootlegs.

2/21/59 USA   **Ritchie Valens** (Del-Fi 1201)
That's My Little Suzie; In a Turkish Town; Come On, Let's Go; Donna; Boney-Maronie; Ooh, My Head; La Bamba; Bluebirds Over the Mountain; Hi-Tone; Framed; We Belong Together; Dooby-Dooby Wah.

10/59 (USA)   **Ritchie** (Del-Fi 1206) / (London HA 2390)*
*(UK) 10/61   Stay Beside Me; Cry, Cry, Cry; Big Baby Blues; The Paddiwack Song; My Darling Is Gone; Hurry Up; Little Girl; Now You're Gone; Fast Freight; Ritchie's Blues; Rockin' All Night.

12/31/60 (USA)   **Ritchie Valens In Concert At Pacoima Junior High** (Del-Fi 1214)[3]
Come On, Let's Go (different version); From Beyond; Donna; Summertime Blues; La Bamba; Rhythm Song; Guitar Instrumental; Malagueña; Rock Lil' Darlin'; Let's Rock & Roll.

4/20/63 (USA)   **Ritchie Valens' Greatest Hits** (Del-Fi 1225) (London HA 8196)* (The UK release was also reissued in
*(UK) 2/65   February, 1967, on President PTL 1001.)
Donna; La Bamba; Come On, Let's Go; We Belong Together; Bluebirds Over the Mountain; In a Turkish Town; Stay Beside Me; Cry, Cry, Cry; Hurry Up; Rockin' All Night; From Beyond; Malagueña

early 1964? (USA)   **Ritchie Valens, His Greatest Hits, Vol. II** (Del-Fi 1247)
La Bamba; Donna; Cry, Cry, Cry; Rockin' All Night; Now You're Gone; Let's Rock & Roll; That's My Little Suzie; Framed; Dooby Dooby Wah; Ooh, My Head; Rock Lil' Darlin'; Boney-Maronie.

---

[3]There are also two bootlegs of this LP: an Australian release (Prims PRLP 1214), date unknown, and a German release from Hamburg, West Germany (D-Del-Fi 1214), release date 2/77. The West German release has a different cover, a promotional shot taken of Ritchie from the movie "Go Johnny Go."

late 60's? (USA)

The Original Ritchie Valens (Guest Star G1469) (Stereo)
Donna; Little Girl; Now You're Gone; Fast Freight; Ritchie's Blues; Rockin' All Night; Rock Little Donna; Hurry Up; Hi-Tone; We Belong Together (cut-off).
(This is a very poor pressing. My guess is that this release may be a bootleg.)

late 60's? (USA)

The Original La Bamba (Guest Star G1484) (Stereo)
Come On, Let's Go; That's My Little Suzie; In a Turkish Town; Ooh, My Head; Dooby Dooby Wah; Cry, Cry, Cry; Big Baby Blues; Paddiwack Song; My Darling Is Gone.
(Same quality pressing as G1469.)

mid 60's? (USA)

Ritchie Valens and Jerry Cole (Crown 336)
Little Girl; Cry, Cry, Cry; Paddiwack Song; Hurry Up; That's My Little Suzie. Other tracks by Jerry Cole.
(Poor quality recording and pressing.)

early 70's? (USA)

Ritchie Valens' Greatest Hits (MGM GAS 117)
Reissue of the Del-Fi 1225 contents.

1973 (Holland)

We Still Remember (T.O.M. 536) (bootleg)
Contains Rock Little Donna; the demo of That's My Little Suzie; Let's Rock & Roll; songs of other late artists.

1974 (UK)

Rock Lil' Darlin' (Joy 254)
Framed; Come On, Let's Go; That's My Little Suzie; Rock Lil' Darlin'; Rockin' All Night; Boney-Maronie; Dooby Dooby Wah; Now You're Gone; Cry, Cry, Cry; Ooh, My Head.

1970's? (West Germany)

Ritchie Valens (D Ariola-Eurodisc 913078)[4]
Donna; We Belong Together; From Beyond; Stay Beside Me; Bluebirds Over the Mt.; In a Turkish Town; Malagueña; La Bamba; Come On, Let's Go; Rockin' All Night; Cry, Cry, Cry; Hurry Up.

[4]Although this record is reputedly from West Germany, the information on the label is written in both French and Italian!

LP's (33's)

7/79 (UK)

Ritchie Valens (London/Decca HAR 8535)
La Bamba; Bluebirds Over the Mt.; Stay Beside Me; Big Baby Blues; Cry, Cry, Cry; Ritchie's Blues; Now You're Gone; Hurry Up; Paddiwack Song; Come On, Let's Go; Ooh, My Head; Donna; Fast Freight; Little Girl; My Darling Is Gone; We Belong Together; That's My Little Suzie; Rockin' All Night.

1979 (Australia)

Same title, songs and record no. as above, but Australian pressing.

late 70's? (USA)

Greatest Hits (Mirwood—numbers and contents unknown)
May be a bootleg.

late 70's? (USA)

Radio transcriptions (Ritchie Valens), Part I (RT 1)
Radio transcriptions (Ritchie Valens), Part II (RT 2)
Little is known by the author about these transcriptions. However, they may have been recorded especially for Army overseas radio.

7/81(USA)

The History of Ritchie Valens (Rhino 2798)
This three LP boxed set is the reproduction of the original three Del-Fi releases especially arranged by manager Bob Keane. The contents also contain a booklet on Valens' life.

7/81 (USA)

The Best of Ritchie Valens (Rhino 200)
La Bamba; Bluebirds Over the Mt.; In a Turkish Town; Ooh, My Head; Paddiwack Song; Stay Beside Me; Malagueña; Come On, Let's Go; Donna; Fast Freight; We Belong Together; That's My Little Suzie; Hurry Up; Little Girl.

1981 (West Germany)

The Best of Ritchie Valens (Line Series LLP 5132 AS) (in collaboration with Bob Keane and Rhino Records)
La Bamba; Bluebirds Over the Mt.; We Belong Together; Ooh, My Head; Paddiwack Song; Stay Beside Me; In a Turkish Town; Come On, Let's Go; Donna; That's My Little Suzie; Rockin' All Night; Rock Little Donna; Cry, Cry, Cry; Fast Freight; Hurry Up; Little Girl.

1981 (West Germany)

I Remember Ritchie Valens—His Greatest Hits (Strand 6.24884)
Contents same as Del-Fi 1225, minus From Beyond.

1981 (West Germany)

Ritchie Valens (Line LLP 5135 AS) (in collaboration with Bob Keane and Rhino Records)
Contents same as Del-Fi 1201.

1981 (West Germany)

Ritchie (Line LLP 5139 AS) (in collaboration with Bob Keane and Rhino Records)
Contents same as Del-Fi 1206.

1981 (West Germany)

Ritchie Valens In Concert At Pacoima Junior High
(Line LLP 5143 AS) (in collaboration with Bob Keane and Rhino Records)
Contents same as Del-Fi 1214.

1981? (Canada)

Ritchie Valens (Phonodisc-Canada)
This Canadian release is probably in collaboration with Bob Keane and Rhino Records, though it is not definitely known. Contents same as Del-Fi 1201. Also, there is a strong possibility that the other two original releases, plus the "Best Of . . ." album have been released in Canada under Phonodisc.

1982 (West Germany)

The Story of Rock & Roll—Ritchie Valens (President 27 683 XAT)
May be reissue of earlier President recording.

1982 (UK)

Those Oldies But Goodies From Del-Fi (Ace CH 63)
Contains Come On, Let's Go, Ooh, My Head, and Fast Freight, along with cuts from Chan Romero, the Carlos Brothers, Bill Lewis, the Defenders, and the Addrissi Brothers.

1983 (USA)

The History of Latino Rock, Vol. I (Rhino RNLP 061)
Contains La Bamba and Donna, along with cuts from various other Latino rock artists.

12" Extended Play (33)

Label	No.	Title (Contents)	Date	Country
Del-Fi (Rhino)	907	La Bamba/Come On, Let's Go/We Belong Together	7/81	USA

Tribute Records (45's)

Recordings that mention Ritchie Valens in tribute.

Label	No.	Title/Artist(s)	Date	Country
UALP	9959[5]	Three Stars (Eddie Cochran)	2/5/59	USA
Crest	1057	Three Stars (Tommy Dee)	2/3/59	USA
King	5192[6]	Three Stars (Ruby Wright)	2/59	USA
Parlophone	R-4556	Three Stars (Ruby Wright)	1959	UK
Skoop	1050	Buddy, Big Bopper and Ritchie (Loretta Thompson)	3/30/59	USA
Energy	105	Gone Too Soon (Chuck Travis)	1959?	USA
D	1052	Gold Records in the Snow (Bennie Barnes)	4/6/59	USA
Ace	558	The Great Tragedy (Hershel Almond)	1959?	USA
Cub	9026	Three Young Men (Lee Davis)	1959	USA
Beat	1008	Three Friends (Scott Wood)	1959	USA
Kapp	524	Teenage Heaven (Johnny Cymbal)	5/63	USA
Trend	106	The Stage (Waylon Jennings)	1960's	USA
Negram	26206	The Story of Buddy Holly (Familee)	1978	Holland

[5] This recording was originally meant to be released as a 45 single in February 1959. However, there were technical problems that delayed the release of the song, which did not appear until later on an LP, long after Cochran's death in 1960.

[6] Also available in stereo on King 45-S-5192.

Recordings that are a tribute to Ritchie specifically:

D	1047[7]	Ballad of Donna and Peggy Sue	3/59?	USA
Pop	1103	Now That You're Gone/Lost Without You (Donna Ludwig)	1959	USA
Unart	29081	A Letter to Donna (Kittens)	1959	USA

Miscellaneous Recordings[8]

Vogue/Coral	PRU 24047	Bridge of Sighs/Scene of the Crime (Ritchie Valens)	n.d.	France
Festival (EP)	?	B'wana Niña/16 Candles + two unknown pieces (Valens)	n.d.	Australia

---

[7] D 1047 has been counterfeited.

[8] There is a question as to whether these recordings exist. However, there is no proof to the contrary. There also supposedly exists a twelve minute studio version of "Ooh, My Head" (5/58), a second version of "Let's Rock & Roll," and some recordings of Ritchie in concert in Honolulu. The author personally knows of an extended version of the Pacoima Junior High School concert, owned by Gail Smith, and recordings of the Silhouettes, owned by William Jones; also, there are some recordings of Ritchie in concert in Honolulu and a concert at San Fernando High School. To date, none of these recordings has been discovered and/or made available.

Addendum

In October 1986, Rhino re-released its "Best of Ritchie Valens" album (Rhino 200) as part of its Golden Archive Series (RNLP 70178). In early 1987, the original three Del-Fi albums (1201, 1206, 1214) were also re-released by Rhino. In addition, Bob Keane has released on Del-Fi a 12" EP dance single (DF 1287) titled "La Bamba '87" which contains four new mixes of the song using the original vocal track and adding female back-up vocals, synthesizers, and other electronic effects.

This poster was used for all the concerts of the Winter Dance Party tour. This one is from the Surf Ballroom in Clear Lake, Iowa, the last concert for Ritchie, Buddy Holly, and the Big Bopper (Feb. 2, 1959). Photo: Bill Griggs collection.

Scene of the plane crash, Albert Juhl farm, near Clear Lake, Iowa, morning of February 3, 1959. Photo: Elwin Musser.

This professional shot of Ritchie was placed in the San Fernando High School yearbook for 1960, the year Ritchie would have graduated. Memorial statement with Ritchie's autograph. Photo: S. Guitarez/B. Mendheim collection.

Announcement for rosary and funeral arrangements for Ritchie. Copy provided by Gil Rocha.

The simple gravestone marking the burial site of Ritchie Valens at San Fernando Mission Cemetery. Photo: B. Mendheim.

Friends and family of Ritchie at the memorial service to commemorate his 18th birthday, held at San Fernando Mission cemetery, May 13, 1959. Among those attending are (kneeling) G. Rocha (second from left), Gail Smith (center left), Donna Fox (center right), Lillian Beckett (second from right), and (standing, center back) Ernestine Reyes. Photo: Gil Rocha collection.

Donna (Ludwig/Fox) holding portrait of Ritchie at the 18th birthday memorial service, May 13, 1959. Photo: Gil Rocha collection.

Cover sleeve for the Limited Valens Memorial Series EP (Del-Fi 101), with autographed photo of Ritchie. Photo: S. Guitarez/B. Mendheim collection.

Ritchie's main guitars: (left) Gibson and (right) Fender Stratocaster. Photo taken in 1970 by B. Mendheim.

A view of the Ritchie Valens mural at Pacoima Junior High School, Pacoima, CA, which was dedicated on June 15, 1985. Photo: B. Mendheim.

Mrs. Valenzuela (Ritchie's mother) with daughters Connie (left) and Irma (right) in front of the Ritchie Valens mural at Pacoima Junior High School. Photo: B. Mendheim.

Lou Diamond Phillips plays Ritchie Valens in Columbia Pictures' "La Bamba," a New Visions Production, written and directed by Luis Valdez. Photo: Copyright © 1986 Columbia Pictures Industries, Inc. All rights reserved. Courtesy of Columbia Pictures.

Esai Morales (right) has the key role of Ritchie's half-brother, Bob Morales, in the film "La Bamba." Photo: Copyright © 1986 Columbia Pictures Industries, Inc. All rights reserved. Courtesy of Columbia Pictures.